THE
LANGUAGE
OF
FLOWERS
A Miscellany

BY MANDY KIRKBY

WITH A FOREWORD BY
VANESSA DIFFENBAUGH

MACMILLAN

First published 2011 by Macmillan
an imprint of Pan Macmillan,
a division of Macmillan Publishers Limited
Pan Macmillan, 20 New Wharf Road, London N1 9RR
Basingstoke and Oxford
Associated companies throughout the world

www.panmacmillan.com

ISBN 978-0-230-75963-3

Copyright © Mandy Kirkby 2011
Foreword © Vanessa Diffenbaugh 2011

The right of Mandy Kirkby to be identified as the author of this work
has been asserted by her in accordance with the Copyright, Designs and
Patents Act 1988.

9 8 7 6 5 4 3

A CIP catalogue record for this book is available from the British Library.

Designed by seagulls.net
Cover design and illustrations by Katie Tooke
Printed and bound in Italy by Printer Trento S.R.L.

Visit **www.panmacmillan.com** to read more about all our books and to
buy them. You will also find features, author interviews and news of any
author events, and you can sign up for e-newsletters so that you're always
first to hear about our new releases.

CONTENTS

Foreword

Flowers do speak a language,
clear and intelligible. Observe them, reader,
love them, linger over them and ask your own heart
if they do not speak affection, benevolence and piety.

In every culture and throughout time, flowers have been central to the human experience. Whether growing wild or in carefully tended gardens, blooming in works of art or written into the pages of great literature, flowers have always surrounded and supported us. They appear in our most significant rituals and traditions all around the globe: from east to west; from ancient civilization to the present day; when we hope or pray, love or mourn; we do it with flowers in our hands.

But why do flowers play such a significant role in our lives? What mystery do they represent and reveal? And how does our deep connection to flowers show itself? In every season and in every country, the answers to these questions are different.

In the Indian state of Uttarakhand, where the Ganga River drops out of the Himalayas and into the valley, a ceremony takes place every evening at sunset. While prayers buzz through a crackling PA system, pilgrims to the holy site of Har Ki Pauri (Steps of the Lord) fill banana-leaf boats with flowers – roses, orchids, tulsi and marigolds – then place a lit candle among the petals and float the fragrant bundle down the river with a hope, a prayer, or a wish.

Across the globe from the Ganga River, in Mexico and through-out Latin America, *cempasuchil* – bright orange marigolds – grow. *Cempasuchil*, the flower the Aztecs used to remember the deceased, is cultivated in preparation for *Dia de los Muertos* (Day of the Dead). Families plant seeds and tend their gardens, thinking of the loved ones they have lost as they watch the marigolds sprout, grow and finally blossom. The brilliant orange flowers are believed to help guide the souls of loved ones home, and for a single day the Mexican people find comfort in having the spirits of their loved ones with them once again.

Every spring in Japan, citizens listen to the weather-bureau forecast the *Sakura Zensen* (the cherry blossom front). At the height of the blossom, *Hanami* (flower viewing) festivals take place all across the country, with friends and family gathering for tea or lunch under the pink canopies. Festivities often go well into the night, with music and paper lanterns illuminating the trees. While the celebrations are joyful, they are brief: cherry trees are in full bloom for two weeks at the most. The perfect, delicate flowers have come to represent the essence of life itself – shockingly beautiful and heartbreakingly fleeting.

In France on May Day, there is a similar focus on a single flower: lily of the valley. This delicate white flower, which grows as a row of bell-shaped blossoms nestled in long green leaves, is often referred to as *porte-bonheur* – literally, 'bringer of happiness'. Every street corner overflows with the flower: florists have huge outdoor displays of the plant; people come in from the countryside to sell plants they've grown in their garden or harvested in the woods. Makeshift stands support heaps of flowers in bundles held together with a ribbon. The lily of the valley is so profuse that even the metro has a tinge of springtime sweetness, as commuters clutch fragrant bouquets of the delicate white flowers.

And then, of course, there are the wedding ceremonies: from England to the United States and beyond, flowers play a part in every aspect of this important tradition, from the bridal bouquet to the centrepieces. At many weddings a flower girl precedes the bride, clutching a basket of rose petals and scattering them down the aisle. The petals she drops are meant to create a path of love and beauty that will carry the bride into her new life as a married woman.

In Asia, the Americas, Japan and Europe, these traditions have remained constant for hundreds of years. It is astonishing to realize that while everything else around us has changed – housing, transportation, technology, methods and styles of communication – flowers and their traditions have remained the same. We grow them, we study them, and we give them – to guests, to hosts, to loved ones, in times of joy and sorrow, awe and appreciation. While both the traditions and the significance of the flowers vary from region to region, always there are flowers, and always there is the desire to communicate.

But what is it that we are trying to say, and why do we use flowers to try to say it? What is it about the flower itself that we are drawn to? Is it the simple expression of the cycle of life we so admire: from seed to sapling, to bud to blossom, and back to seed? Is it the courage of the first snowdrop, braving the last days of winter to push through the frozen ground? Or is it the sweet fragrance of the rose – a scent that physically changes our brain chemistry, bringing a rush of warmth and joy?

It is these questions that have spawned symbolic flower languages in almost every culture since ancient times. From the nature worship of early religions to Greek and Roman mythology, humans have assigned floral symbols to Gods and deities, prophets and saints. In the Christian faith the Virgin Mary is forever associated with the white lily, from the story of the Apostles opening her casket and finding only roses and lilies; in the Hindu religion, deities' eyes are often represented as flower blossoms, looking out with compassion and wisdom; the Buddha is frequently depicted sitting on an open lotus blossom, the symbol of full enlightenment.

The Victorian era was the great age of the flower garden and of all things horticultural, and so it is not surprising that flower symbolism became particularly elaborate at this time. At the heart of the Victorians' love of flowers was their strong and direct connection with nature, much more so and in quite a different way than our connection today. The majority of the population still lived on the land, nature itself was much more abundant and fruitful, and the notion that God spoke to man through the natural world, conveying messages, particularly moral ones, was an intrinsic part of everyday thinking. Increased trade and travel brought a wealth of new and exotic species from the East and the Americas, which were cultivated in hothouses and delighted over.

The origin of the western language of flowers, an intricate system of floral symbolism in which each flower is assigned a specific meaning, is thought to have been inspired by the Turkish custom of *sélam* – a method of communicating through flowers and other objects. In the Turkish tradition, the objects did not carry a symbolic meaning; rather, the recipient would decode the message based on guessing words that rhymed with the object.

The idea of the *sélam* was popularized in Europe by the *Turkish Embassy Letters* of Lady Mary Wortley Montagu, which were published after her death in 1763. Her letters described the *sélam* as a method of communication between lovers in which it was possible to send messages 'without ever inking your fingers', and gave examples of their meanings. She did not call this method of communication a language of flowers, nor did she suggest the creation of a western equivalent. Yet when the letters were popularized in the nineteenth century, western culture – already flower obsessed – extracted from the list of objects that which they found to be romantic (flowers), got rid of the rest (metal, foodstuffs, dragon's blood, etc.) and began to assign definitions to each flower based on literature, poetry, art and horticulture.

The first western language of flowers dictionary, *Le Langage des Fleurs*, written in 1819 by Charlotte de Latour (a pseudonym), was so popular that it created a minor industry. Countless numbers of illustrated floral dictionaries sprouted up in France and across Europe, eventually making their way overseas to America. Often written by journalists and editors of popular magazines, flower dictionaries were targeted at genteel young ladies, for whom the association of flowers and romantic love was immensely appealing. Their contents were all very similar: an alphabetical list of flowers with their symbolic meanings, explanations as to how certain flowers obtained their meanings – usually from Classical mythology, folklore, medieval and Arthurian-type legends – flower poetry, examples of bouquet combinations and the messages they convey, and more often than not something called the Floral Oracle, a description of various fortune-telling games using flowers. Luxurious bindings, unusual sizes and beautiful illustrations made each floral dictionary unique.

There is little evidence that the Victorians actually used the language of flowers in a practical way; they didn't send continuous streams of bouquets to each other, but rather the books were meant for the 'centre' (coffee) table and were to be studied, indulged in, and played as a game; every young lady wanted to be well-versed in the meanings of flowers. And though they didn't spend hours coding secret bouquets, the Victorians did set great store by flowers and used them extensively in everyday life, much more so than today. Bouquets as love tokens *were* sent, carnation buttonholes were extremely popular, and women wore flowers a great deal – in their hair, on their evening gowns, or tucked into a bodice. Flower symbolism was important and was applied to all the major occasions in life: roses, violets and forget-me-nots during courtship, orange blossoms at weddings, and wreaths of cypress at funerals and as grave ornaments. From popular culture to high art, poets, painters, novelists, writers of children's books, magazine journalists, composers and lyricists all played with the idea in their work. Some took the language of flowers seriously, others poked gentle fun at it, but there is no doubt that it was a major phenomenon. One of the great paintings of the age was John Everett Millais's depiction of the drowned Ophelia, surrounded by flowers and drenched in symbolism: 'There's Rosemary, that's for remembrance; . . . and there is Pansies, that's for thoughts.'

As the Victorian era came to an end, the popularity of the language of flowers began to fade. Queen Victoria died in 1901; little more than a decade later, the world was at war. The two world wars changed the way we related to each other as human beings for ever; the emerging technological age changed the way we related to the world around us for ever. Victorian sentiment – allowing emotions to influence decisions – became referred to with some distaste as 'sentimentality' and became frowned upon. The era of the logical, scientific mind was ushered in. Huge developments in science and manufacturing prevailed, and in less than a century we had moved from horseback to high-speed trains to airplanes, from the pony express to the cellular phone, from Morse code to the Internet. But even as tastes and trends changed dramatically in the twentieth century, flowers themselves never went out of fashion. Flowers continued to be a way for humans to express complex emotions: World War I is inextricably linked to the poppy; the song 'where have all the flowers gone' stirs up emotion for anyone who lived through the Vietnam War.

Now, in the current information era, we know more than we've ever known. Science and technology have advanced to the point where not only do we understand more about the world, but all of our collective understanding is gathered in a single, if virtual, space. As a species we continue to grow and change, to come up with new ways to communicate and new things to say. We call instead of knocking on doors, or text if we are too nervous to call. If we are uncertain about what we want to say, we can double-check facts on a screen or get a second opinion from an ever-present social network. But has any of this helped us to communicate more effectively? Are any of our technological methods of declaring love more meaningful than a single orange tulip in a blue glass vase, growing taller in the direction of the light? Is anything more perfect than a banana-leaf boat full of flowers floating down a river to express our devotion to the divine? Is anything more useful than a bed of bright orange marigolds to help us find our way home?

We plant, we nurture, we grow and we give, different flowers for different moments in time, but all for the same purpose: to say that which cannot be said, and to say it with beauty and with grace.

Vanessa Diffenbaugh

Fifty Featured Flowers

anemone ✲ basil ✲ camellia

Canterbury bells ✲ carnation ✲ chamomile

cherry blossom ✲ chrysanthemum ✲ cypress

daffodil ✲ dahlia ✲ daisy ✲ eglantine

forget-me-not ✲ geranium ✲ hazel ✲ heliotrope

holly ✲ hyacinth ✲ iris ✲ ivy ✲ larkspur

lavender ✲ lilac ✲ lily ✲ lily of the valley

marigold ✲ mignonette ✲ mistletoe ✲ moss

myrtle ✲ nasturtium ✲ orange blossom ✲ orchid

pansy ✲ passionflower ✲ peppermint ✲ periwinkle

poppy ✲ rose ✲ rosemary ✲ snowdrop

sunflower ✲ thistle ✲ tulip ✲ verbena ✲ violet

wallflower ✲ water lily ✲ weeping willow

Anemone *(Anemone)*

ANEMONE

Forsaken

These beautiful, fragile flowers come from the Near East and the Mediterranean, and were first brought to Britain at the end of the sixteenth century. In Greece, anemones carpet the hillsides and olive groves in springtime with their brilliant red, white, pink and purple blooms. Their name comes from the Greek *anemos*, meaning 'the wind', because their delicate flowers appear to open in a gentle breeze, but are so short-lived, like a breath of wind.

The anemone has come to be associated with the story of the lovers Aphrodite and Adonis. Aphrodite, the Greek goddess of love, was besotted with this beautiful youth, but he was fatally wounded by a wild boar and died in her arms. She sprinkled nectar on his blood, from which sprang the vivid red anemone. Abandonment, and love that is fleeting and will not last, are symbolized by this flower.

COME HARRIET! SWEET IS THE HOUR

Come Harriet! sweet is the hour,
Soft Zephyrs breathe gently around,
The anemone's night-boding flower,
Has sunk its pale head on the ground.

'Tis thus the world's keenness hath torn,
Some mild heart that expands to its blast,
'Tis thus that the wretched forlorn,
Sinks poor and neglected at last. –

The world with its keenness and woe,
Has no charms or attraction for me,
Its unkindness with grief has laid low,
The heart which is faithful to thee.

The high trees that wave past the moon,
As I walk in their umbrage with you,
All declare I must part with you soon,
All bid you a tender adieu! –

Then Harriet! dearest, farewell,
You and I, love, may ne'er meet again;
These woods and these meadows can tell
How soft and how sweet was the strain. –

Percy Bysshe Shelley
WRITTEN IN 1810 FOR HIS FIRST WIFE, HARRIET WESTBROOK

A small vase of anemones makes an appearance in William Holman Hunt's 1853 painting *The Awakening Conscience*. Hunt's subject is that of a young gentleman visiting his mistress in the house in which he has installed her. She is sitting with him at the piano when she is suddenly stricken with remorse and rises from his lap. The room is full of objects symbolic of her predicament, including a cat that has caught a bird under the table, a sheet of music of Thomas Moore's 'Oft in the Stilly Night' – a song about former innocence and present despair – and the anemones in the vase on the piano, which hint that the affair will not last and can only end in sorrow.

BASIL

Hate

It was the Ancient Greeks who first associated basil with that fierce emotion and the misfortune that swiftly follows on. They saw in the basil flower, with its pointed double lip, a resemblance to the head of the legendary basilisk, the king of the serpents. He could kill with a single glance, and hatred was said to have the eyes of a basilisk. A curious and ancient fancy warned that scorpions took shelter under a basil pot, and a sprig of basil placed under a pot would breed a scorpion.

This sweet and aromatic plant was first grown in Britain in the sixteenth century, when it became a favourite kitchen and strewing herb. The Victorians considered it too strongly flavoured for their tastes, and grew it in the hothouse, where it was valued for its creamy flowers and deep and musky scent. Those who were wealthy enough to make the Grand Tour would have been familiar with this plant, and perhaps would have brought a few seeds back home with them.

One of the most startling of Victorian paintings is William Holman Hunt's *Isabella and the Pot of Basil*, painted in 1868 and inspired by John Keats's poem of the same name. The story of Isabella is a gruesome one: her lover, Lorenzo, is murdered by her brothers and buried in the forest. On finding his body, Isabella removes the head, places it in a large pot, covers it with earth, plants it with basil and waters it with her tears. The painting shows a mournful Isabella draped over a large majolica pot, in which grows a profusion of basil. The pot sits on a table covered with a cloth embroidered with roses and passionflowers, the emblems for love and faith.

from ISABELLA; OR THE POT OF BASIL

Then in a silken scarf, – sweet with the dews
Of precious flowers pluck'd in Araby,
And divine liquids come with odorous ooze
Through the cold serpent-pipe refreshfully, –
She wrapp'd it up; and for its tomb did choose
A garden-pot, wherein she laid it by,
And cover'd it with mould, and o'er it set
Sweet Basil, which her tears kept ever wet.

And she forgot the stars, the moon, and sun,
And she forgot the blue above the trees,
And she forgot the dells where waters run,
And she forgot the chilly autumn breeze;
She had no knowledge when the day was done,
And the new morn she saw not: but in peace
Hung over her sweet Basil evermore,
And moisten'd it with tears unto the core.

JOHN KEATS

Basil (*Ocimum basilicum*)

Camellia *(Camellia)*

Camellia

My Destiny Is in Your Hands

Camellia-petal
fell in silent dawn
Spilling
A water jewel.

Matsuo Bashō, seventeenth-century Haiku poet

The camellia is an evergreen bush, and is known as the Empress of Winter as it blooms during the long dark months of the year, bringing us lightness and gaiety. In Japan, where it grows in the wild, it is especially revered. It produces glorious flowers, striking and feminine, which appear as double or single blooms, in colours from pure white through to dusky pink and deep red. A flower of singular beauty, the camellia speaks of love, strong and all-embracing, of destinies inextricably linked.

The flower is named after a Jesuit missionary and botanist called Georg Kamel who brought the camellia to Europe from east Asia in the early eighteenth century. It was grown in the hothouse and became an exotic luxury, and by the mid-nineteenth century it was one of the most sought-after flowers. The Victorians were especially captivated by the white camellia, luscious and dramatic against beautiful shiny green leaves. It was the belle of winter flowers, gracing dinner parties, balls and concert rooms; gleaming out in rosy crimson streaks from flaxen hair, or showing off its depth of spotless whiteness among dark braids of brown or black.

At fancy-dress balls, girls would come as camellias, and there was no waltz or cotillion danced where a lady did not clasp a bouquet of them. A posy of a white camellia surrounded by a band of violets and a fringe of scented geranium leaves presented to a lady would be immensely flattering, and a bridal bouquet of the flowers a sensation.

A pink and a red camellia appear in John William Waterhouse's *Camellias*, where they adorn the hair of a young woman. Waterhouse painted many portraits of women, as mythological characters or as damsels from Arthurian legends, all the while trying to capture his vision of idealized womanhood, but perhaps this portrait is one of the loveliest, the woman straightforwardly portrayed, the camellia flower a simple expression of feminine beauty and love.

CANTERBURY BELLS

Constancy

Fair are the bells of this bright-flowering weed.
CONSTANCE NADEN

The name of the flower group to which this lovely plant belongs is *Campanula*, meaning 'little bell', referring to the shape of its striking blue or white flowers. It was given its common name from the bells the pilgrims carried as they made their weary way to Thomas à Becket's shrine, and this connection with devotion has made it an emblem of faith and constancy, especially religious faith.

The plant can grow tall, its stems shooting up to two or three feet high, and when it blooms it is a glorious sight. From July to October it is covered from top to bottom with beautiful large flowers, and the Victorians put this abundance to good use by growing it in pots and garden borders for summer display. A few blooms plucked off and tucked into a lady's hair would make for a simple decoration, or the potted plant presented to a curate's wife an entirely appropriate gift.

A much-loved painting of the time was John Everett Millais's *A Huguenot on St Bartholomew's Day*, exhibited to great acclaim in 1852. The painting was inspired by a story from the St Bartholomew's Day Massacre of 1572, and shows a Catholic girl and her Protestant lover embracing in a garden. The girl is trying to bind a white cloth around his arm in order to identify him as Catholic, thus saving him from persecution. While his one hand tries to pull away the cloth, the other holds the head of his beloved. Growing prominently by their feet is a Canterbury bell, and ivy ('fidelity') trails up and along the wall behind them.

Millais often used the language of flowers in his paintings, and in *The Blind Girl* he called upon another bellflower, the pale blue, fragile harebell. A blind beggar girl has stopped by the roadside, waiting for a passing shower to clear; behind her is a double rainbow and in the grass by her hand a small clump of harebells. The expression on her face is one of patience and stoicism: the emblem for harebell is 'resignation'.

> *Hope is like a harebell trembling from its birth,*
> *Love is like a rose the joy of all the earth;*
> *Faith is like a lily lifted high and white,*
> *Love is like a lovely rose the world's delight;*
> *Harebells and sweet lilies show a thornless growth,*
> *But the rose with all its thorns excels them both.*

CHRISTINA ROSSETTI

Canterbury Bells (*Campanula medium*)

Carnation *(Dianthus caryophyllus)*

CARNATION

Pink – I Will Never Forget You ❋ *Red – My Heart Breaks*
White – Sweet and Lovely ❋ *Yellow – Disdain*
Striped – I Cannot Be with You

This delicate and modest flower, which blooms at the height
of summer when the weather is kind and gentle, is from the
family *Dianthus*, which also includes pinks (*pure love*) and Sweet
Williams (*gallantry*). The carnation's perfume is delicious and
spicy, like the scent of cloves. It was originally a wild plant of
southern Europe, introduced to England by the Normans, but the
Victorians loved the cultivated flower, breeding more and more
varieties in endless variants of colour and form.

The word carnation comes from the Latin *caro*, meaning
'flesh', and is a nod towards the delicate pink of its petals, but
the name *Dianthus* derives from the Greek *Dios*, 'of Zeus', and
anthos, meaning 'flower'. Thus the name means Zeus's flower.
The carnation has always been associated with the higher things,
with fine emotions and love and marriage. Many Renaissance
paintings show betrothed couples holding a carnation.

A red carnation might be presented as a strong avowal of love;
a white carnation placed on a lady's breakfast tray would be an
affectionate and tender gesture. It became the fashion to give buttonholes to gentlemen at dinner parties, tucked under the napkin or
sent in on trays before everyone sat at table. Traditionally, the eldest
daughter would help each guest to choose, perhaps the wonder-
fully scented 'Souvenir de la Malmaison' or the lovely new variety
'Mrs Sinkins' with its ragged white petals and sweet fragrance.

Oscar Wilde wore a green carnation in his buttonhole to the opening night of *Lady Windermere's Fan* in 1892, with mauve gloves. He asked friends in the audience to wear one too, to be obtained from Goodyear the florist in the Royal Arcade in Mayfair. When asked what the carnation meant, he replied, 'Nothing whatever, but that is just what nobody will guess.'

Louisa Anne Twamley, in her 1836 *The Romance of Nature*, warned inattentive young women to use the carnation with care when conveying love messages. She explains why in a chivalric floral ballad entitled 'Carnations and Cavaliers'. The Lady Edith and the knight Sir Rupert are saying good-night, and he presents her with a pink (*pure love*). Inadvertently, she gives him back a carnation – presumably striped – forgetting that:

> *The Pink, by Knight to Ladye given,*
> *Prays her to be his Bride –*
> *The proud carnation answering tells*
> *That fervent prayer's denied.*

And later in the poem:

> *Now, Ladye – when a Cavalier*
> *Presents a chequered PINK,*
> *'Tis time to ascertain, my dear,*
> *His rent roll, you may think.*

> *And then – provided his estate*
> *Don't meet your approbation,*
> *It cannot, surely, be too late*
> *To cut – with a CARNATION.*

CHAMOMILE

Energy in Adversity

'The chamomile bed; the more it is trodden, the more it will spread.'

PROVERB

Chamomile is an unassuming little plant: its flower is daisy like and petite, its foliage light and feathery, its fragrance gentle. But what battles it fights, and how much stronger it is for the undertaking! A flower of grassland and sandy commons, it falls prey to grazing cattle and trampling feet and, in response, it grows lower and tighter: it finds the courage to survive and is all the stronger for it.

The name chamomile is derived from the Greek word *khamaemelon*, meaning 'earth apple', a reference to the plant's fruity fragrance. It is native to Britain, and has been cultivated as both a medicinal herb and a turfing plant for lawns. The chamomile lawn and seat were favourite features of Elizabethan gardens, mossily soft and smelling of apples when sat upon, but only regular clipping and deflowering would achieve a tight sward. It is said that Francis Drake's famous game of bowls was played on a chamomile lawn.

'Chamomylle is very agreeing unto the nature of man, and is good against weariness.'

WILLIAM TURNER, SIXTEENTH-CENTURY BOTANIST

The Victorians knew chamomile as a great cure-all and energy giver. A tea brewed with the flowers would act as a restorative; a distillation of the oil made into a cream and rubbed into the skin or added to bathwater would ease pain and take away fatigue. Brought into the sickroom, a few clippings tied together with fennel fronds and sprigs of peppermint would give strength and encouragement for a swift recovery. In the cottage garden, chamomile even had the reputation of being able to restore to health any sickly plant near which it was grown.

The Camomile, a 1922 novel by Catherine Carswell, follows the struggles of a young woman who wants to be a writer, and who suffers disapproval and setbacks all along the way. The novel is semi-autobiographical: Carswell was brought up by strict Victorian parents, and she rejected the conventional life they had planned for her by becoming a journalist and writer. Her personal life was full of tragedy – a disastrous first marriage and the death of a child – and she too, like her heroine, overcame adversity to achieve her goal.

Chamomile (*Matricaria recutita*)

Cherry Blossom *(Prunus cerasus)*

CHERRY BLOSSOM

Impermanence

A cherry tree in full bloom is one of the most glorious sights of the spring calendar – the effect of its pink or white flowers en masse is almost ethereal. But its splendour is short-lived: the blossom soon falls to the ground in great drifts like snow, and its glory is over. It is a reminder that life is fleeting and time is precious. Enjoy the moment, celebrate its coming, acknowledge its passing without sorrow.

LOVELIEST OF TREES, THE CHERRY NOW

Loveliest of trees, the cherry now
Is hung with bloom along the bough,
And stands about the woodland ride
Wearing white for Eastertide.

Now, of my threescore years and ten,
Twenty will not come again,
And take from seventy springs a score,
It only leaves me fifty more.

And since to look at things in bloom
Fifty springs are little room,
About the woodlands I will go
To see the cherry hung with snow.

A. E. HOUSMAN

The wild cherry has grown in Britain and Europe for hundreds of years, introduced by the Romans from Asia. But it was the Japanese cherry tree, the pink-blossomed sakura, brought over to Europe in the 1860s, that captured the imagination of the Victorians, and from Japan's own language of flowers they borrowed its meaning, 'impermanence'.

The late nineteenth century saw a fashion for all things Japanese, and on many of the imported exotic goods – prints, screens, kimonos and porcelain – cherry blossom was a common motif. Cherry trees were planted in Japanese-style gardens, often complete with tea-house and wooden bridge. Hopeful wishes to a friend for the coming year could be conveyed with a greetings card depicting a spray of blossom alongside a Japanese fan.

In James Tissot's 1864 *La Japonaise au Bain*, a young geisha languishes against the side of a verandah, her exquisite kimono draped open to reveal that she is naked underneath. Cherry blossom winds round the wooden verandah and is tucked into her hair, and the tree in full bloom can be seen through the window. Like the blossom, both her beauty and the pleasure she is offering are transient.

CHRYSANTHEMUM

Truth

The chrysanthemum is an ancient and elegant flower, cultivated for over two thousand years in its native East. The Japanese, who have made it the emblem of their emperor, consider the orderly unfolding of its petals to be symbolic of perfection. In August the blooms appear in great numbers, reflecting the ripeness of the season, the summer's work brought to fruition. The essence of the flower is unravelled just as truth is so often revealed: at first hidden, then brought into the light.

Despite its long and illustrious pedigree, the chrysanthemum did not arrive in Britain until the end of the eighteenth century, when seeds and plants were brought back from China by the ships of the East India Company. By the mid-nineteenth century, at least twenty-four varieties were being grown, and its range of forms – pompom, streaked, ragged, flamboyant or prim – and immense palette of colours, from crisp white to burnt umber, made it a favourite Victorian flower.

The chrysanthemum was often shown at winter parties during the shooting season, when pots of colour in a country-house porch would welcome the guests. In its less flamboyant form it was a popular buttonhole flower: a splash of brightness sitting neatly on a jacket. The white chrysanthemum in a wedding bouquet speaks of the bride's honest and true character.

The flower made grand bedding displays in parks and public places, and a gardening correspondent reported landing at St Paul's wharf one November morning when the fog was 'of true

London character'. Here he caught sight of a glorious bed of chrysanthemums in Temple Gardens, shining through the gloom.

In the 1880s, the French had a craze for these flowers, and a bestselling novel of the time was *Madame Chrysanthème* by Pierre Loti, who drew upon a lifetime of travel for the plots of his exotic romances. The book takes the form of the diary of a French naval officer whose ship docks at Nagasaki to undergo repairs. While waiting to sail again he enters into a temporary 'marriage' with a geisha called Chrysanthème.

from THE LAST CHRYSANTHEMUM

Why should this flower delay so long
To show its tremulous plumes?
Now is the time of plaintive robin-song,
When flowers are in their tombs.

Through the slow summer, when the sun
Called to each frond and whorl
That all he could for flowers was being done,
Why did it not uncurl?

It must have felt that fervid call
Although it took no heed,
Waking but now, when leaves like corpses fall,
And saps all retrocede.

Too late its beauty, lonely thing,
The season's shine is spent,
Nothing remains for it but shivering
In tempests turbulent.

THOMAS HARDY

Chrysanthemum (*Chrysanthemum*)

Cypress *(Cupressus)*

Cypress

Mourning

Henceforth, when mourners grieve, their grief to share,
Emblem of woe, the cypress shall be there.
ANON.

The cypress is a sad and melancholy tree, tall and tapering, reaching up into a dark sky. Its dense evergreen foliage permits no light, and as the sun sets the tree casts long shadows upon the ground like strange phantoms. Its name derives from the ancient Greek tale of Cyparissus, a young boy whose favourite companion was a tame stag. When Cyparissus accidentally kills his beloved stag with a hunting javelin, he prays to Apollo that his mourning might be perpetual, and in answer to his prayers the god turns him into a cypress.

The tree's association with grief and mortality is an old one, and comes from the East, where burial grounds are thickly planted with them, and in Biblical times its sweet-smelling wood was used to make coffins and its branches to line graves. It is also said that the cypress, once cut, will never flourish or grow again.

The Victorians embraced the symbolic meaning of the cypress tree and wove it into their rituals of death and mourning. The tree was planted in cemeteries, forming cypress avenues; it was cut in swathes and would line a coffin, or be strewn across it, its fragrance sweetening the room. To announce a death, branches of cypress and other evergreens, emblems of immortality together, would be wound in a wreath with a black crape ribbon and hung on the door. The cypress combined with marigold (*grief*) would speak of great despair.

Once the funeral had taken place, the cypress would make its final appearance, as a small embossed image on a memorial card, serving as a reminder to the mourners to pray for the soul of the departed. Other symbols – an inverted torch (the extinguishing of life), a broken column, a serpent with its tail in its mouth (immortality) – would reinforce its meaning.

WHEN I AM DEAD, MY DEAREST

When I am dead, my dearest,
Sing no sad songs for me;
Plant thou no roses at my head,
Nor shady cypress tree:
Be the green grass above me
With showers and dewdrops wet;
And if thou wilt, remember,
And if thou wilt, forget.

I shall not see the shadows,
I shall not feel the rain;
I shall not hear the nightingale
Sing on, as if in pain:
And dreaming through the twilight
That doth not rise nor set,
Haply I may remember,
And haply may forget.

CHRISTINA ROSSETTI

Daffodil

New Beginnings

To Daffodils

Fair Daffodils, we weep to see
You haste away so soon;
As yet the early-rising sun
Has not attain'd his noon.
Stay, stay,
Until the hasting day
Has run
But to the even-song;
And, having pray'd together, we
Will go with you along.

Robert Herrick

The lovely golden daffodil is a welcome, heart-lifting sight, as it marks the end of winter and the beginning of a new season. It comes into full flower around Easter time, when thoughts turn towards the renewal of life and the Resurrection. It is also known as the Lent lily or the Easter lily.

The daffodil has grown in Britain in the wild since the sixteenth century, once colouring fields and meadows in great drifts and gradually creeping into cottage gardens. To the Victorians, the daffodil was a flower of the countryside, simple and natural, and had a great deal of folklore associated with it, as well as a host of jolly country names such as 'Butter and Eggs', a reference to the flower's two-tone bright yellow colouring. Children welcomed the daffodil and the new season it proclaimed by singing:

'Daffadowndilly has come to town
In a yellow petticoat and a red gown.'

An Easter postcard depicting a fresh-faced young country girl holding an armful of daffodils might be sent to a valued friend; or a bunch of the flowers purchased from one of the many florists' shops around Covent Garden flower market would brighten up a cold spring day.

The daffodil appears in a very charming series of tiles designed by the artist Walter Crane entitled 'Flora's Train'. Each tile depicts a popular Victorian flower personified as a young nymph, a *fleur animée*. The dark green and the fresh bright yellow of the daffodil tile make it probably the loveliest of them all.

But a more sombre note might prevail in rural areas, where it was said to be unlucky to bring the flowers into the house of anyone who kept poultry, because this would prevent the eggs from hatching. And in some places, Wales in particular, the daffodil was used in the traditional practice of 'flowering the graves' on Palm Sunday. Graves would be cleaned, weeded and whitewashed before being decked with garlands of plants, the paying of respects to the dead. It is said that the connection with mournful and unlucky matters comes from the old story that the name 'daffodil' is said to derive from the medieval Latin *affodilus*, and *asphodelos* in Greek – the asphodel, the plant that grew in the meadows of the underworld.

Daffodil (*Narcissus*)

Dahlia *(Dahlia)*

DAHLIA

Dignity

The regal and stately dahlia was first discovered by Europeans during the Spanish conquest of Mexico in the sixteenth century, where it grew in the gardens of the Aztecs. But it was not until the early nineteenth century, when the society hostess Lady Holland saw the plant growing in Madrid and sent some tubers back home, that it first appeared in English gardens. It is named after the Swedish botanist Andreas Dahl.

An anonymous Victorian poet was inspired to praise the flower's ability to withstand the hardship of its new home, 'though severed from its native clime', and to encourage by its example:

And thus the soul – if fortune cast
Its lot to live in scenes less bright, –
Should bloom amidst the adverse blast: –
Nor suffer sorrow's clouds to blight
Its outward beauty – inward light.
Thus should she live and flourish still,
Though misery's frost might strive to kill
The germ of hope within her quite: –
Thus should she hold each beauty fast,
And bud and blossom to the last.

In Britain in the early nineteenth century, sightings of the dahlia were rare, occasionally glimpsed over the wall of an aristocratic garden, but by the 1830s it had become one of the most fashionable flowers in the country. The Victorians loved it for its sensationally bright colours and immense variety, and it became a great favourite at flower shows. The ideal dahlia was the ball-shaped type: an upright bloom with a tightly packed sphere of petals, sitting straight and composed on its sturdy stem – the perfect floral representation of dignity. A variety called 'Little Dorrit' appeared in the late 1850s, named after Charles Dickens's supremely dignified heroine.

If a lady wished to be the height of fashion and her garden was large enough, a dahlia walk could be planted. Two wide borders would be filled with dahlias of different colours, with a grassy path in between, and guests could walk along it to admire the flowers as they caught the last rays of the warm sun. A bunch of the flowers given to an elderly person, the blooms at their peak in the late-summer months, would be especially heartening as autumn beckoned.

The Impressionist painter Claude Monet loved dahlias and grew them in abundance in his first garden at Argenteuil, often exchanging varieties with fellow enthusiasts the painter Gustave Caillebotte and the novelist Octave Mirbeau. Monet's 1873 painting *The Artist's Garden in Argenteuil (A Corner of the Garden with Dahlias)*, one of several paintings he made of one of his favourite flowers, captures their colour and majesty against an autumn sky.

DAISY

Innocence

Daisies, ye flowers of lowly birth
Embroiderers of the carpet earth.
JOHN CLARE

The daisy was known, in Chaucer's time, as 'the day's eye', because the flower opens in the morning and closes in the evening. For centuries, this sweet and tender everyday flower has been a symbol for innocence and lack of worldliness. In the illuminations in medieval Books of Hours, the daisy stood for contempt for worldly goods and also implied that a person could learn something even from the smallest flower in God's creation. Its association with the purity and simplicity of children comes in part from the ancient Celtic belief that when a child dies at birth, an angel throws a daisy down upon the earth to console the bereft parents.

Victorian children would make daisy chains as an amusement, or to form the garland of a May Day crown; a country maid might thread some through her hair as simple decoration or as an indication of her kind and innocent nature. A young woman might spend an afternoon devouring Charlotte M. Yonge's Victorian bestseller *The Daisy Chain*. This 1856 novel, one of more than a hundred penned by this prolific author, was a gentle saga about a family of motherless children.

But it was as an oracle of the affairs of the heart that the daisy was universally known. The petals would be picked one by one:

'He loves me; he loves me not', and the last petal plucked was the indication of love's measure.

William Morris, the craftsman and writer, disliked the fashionable and flamboyant flowers of the day, much preferring the simple and commonplace. His 'Daisy' pattern wallpaper was the first to be issued by Morris & Co. and was popular for over fifty years. In particular, it was bought for maids' rooms and the bedrooms of young girls.

from TO A MOUNTAIN DAISY
ON TURNING ONE DOWN WITH THE PLOUGH, IN APRIL 1786

Wee, modest, crimson-tipp'd flow'r,
Thou's met me in an evil hour,
For I maun crush amang the Stoure
Thy slender stem:
To spare thee now is past my pow'r,
Thou bonnie gem.

ROBERT BURNS

Daisy (*Bellis*)

Eglantine *(Rosa rubiginosa)*

EGLANTINE

I Wound to Heal

Wild-rose, Sweetbriar, Eglantine,
All these pretty names are mine,
And scent in every leaf is mine,
And a leaf for all is mine,
And the scent – Oh, that's divine!
Happy-sweet and pungent fine,
Pure as dew, and pick'd as wine.

LEIGH HUNT

The eglantine, also called the rose briar or sweet briar, is the wild native European rose, found rambling and trailing in hedgerows and country gardens. The name eglantine comes from the Old French *aiglent*, meaning 'needle', and briar is the Old English word for 'thorny shrub'. The eglantine's flowers, which vary in colour from deep pink to white, smell enchantingly of apple, especially after rainfall. Pleasure and pain as one are signified by this flower.

Although the new roses of the Victorian period – imports from China and France, the hybrids from the nurseryman breeders – were all the fashion, the old eglantine was much loved, grown around a garden trellis or trained along a cottage wall. It had romantic and literary associations with Shakespeare's England and the court of Elizabeth I, whose emblem was the eglantine. Shakespeare's love and knowledge of flora impressed the Victorians, who saw an affection for flowers as a sign of wholesomeness and simplicity.

A number of studies of Shakespeare's flowers were published in the nineteenth century, the most popular being *The Flowers of Shakespeare* by Jane Giraud in 1845. Quotations from the plays and sonnets were accompanied by exquisite floral illustrations. The book would be given as a gift, to be lingered over on sunny afternoons. The eglantine appears several times; here, for example, in the description of Titania's bower:

> *I know a bank where the wild thyme blows,*
> *Where oxlips and the nodding violet grows,*
> *Quite over-canopied with luscious woodbine,*
> *With sweet musk-roses, and with eglantine.*
> *There sleeps Titania sometime of the night,*
> *Lull'd in these flowers with dances and delight.*

FROM *A MIDSUMMER NIGHT'S DREAM*, ACT II, SCENE I

If a Victorian lady happened to be visiting Agnew's galleries in Bond Street in 1890, she could not have failed to notice the profusion of eglantines in Edward Burne-Jones's 'Briar Rose' cycle of paintings, which were being exhibited there. The paintings depict scenes from the fairy tale *The Sleeping Beauty*, in which a princess pricks her finger on a spinning wheel and falls asleep, along with her court, for a hundred years. A forest of briars springs up, its deadly thorns protecting them from the outside world. The final painting in the cycle, *The Rose Bower*, shows the sleeping princess: the model was Burne-Jones's daughter Margaret, who had married two years earlier, much to his distress. He adored his daughter and found her growing into womanhood unbearable. He shows Margaret as a beautiful damsel, safely hidden from the world and the prince – and he never lets us see her wake up.

FORGET-ME-NOT

Forget Me Not

That blue and bright-eyed flow'ret of the brook,
Hope's gentle gem, the sweet forget-me-not.
COLERIDGE

The name of this pretty and delicate flower, which enamels riverbanks and garden borders with its miniature sky-blue petals, speaks of the human longing for loyalty and lastingness. Its name comes from a German folk tale about a couple who, on the eve of their marriage, take a walk by the banks of the Danube. The young bride admires a cluster of the flowers, and her fiancé goes forward to pick them for her, but falls into the river. Before he is carried away by the turbulent waters, he throws the flowers at the feet of his betrothed, crying, '*Vergiss mein nicht!*'

The forget-me-not is native to Britain but its name was not used until the nineteenth century. It caught on very quickly, almost certainly popularized by Samuel Taylor Coleridge, who had travelled in Germany and would have been familiar with that country's folklore.

The flower was used as a simple and uncomplicated expression of love, and its sentiment appealed to everyone. Combined with roses, violets and pansies and a delicate slip of lace as a backing, it made a perfect Valentine bouquet. A Valentine card of Cupid framed by a forget-me-not heart might be sent by return. If a beloved was a soldier away on service, a locket engraved with a forget-me-not flower and containing a lock of hair would serve as love's reminder. The little flowers appeared on china and on writing paper, were embroidered on slippers and reproduced in velvet to pin on ladies' bonnets and children's caps. A forget-me-not silver brooch with the initials of a loved one would make a poignant memento mori.

A Victorian lady, wishing to be in the thoughts of a valued and distant friend, might send her the popular *Forget-Me-Not Annual*. These modest little books, whose typical contents might include poems by Lord Byron and John Clare, stories by Walter Scott and Mary Shelley, articles on flowers, birds and country churchyards, were considered indispensable in middle-class drawing rooms.

The very name is Love's own poetry,
Born of the heart, and of the eye begot,
Nursed amid sighs and smiles of constancy,
And ever breathing – 'Love! forget me not.'

The Reverend Francis Kilvert wrote in his diary on 4 September 1874 of finding a bookmark on which was embroidered in silk the words 'Forget-me-not'. It was a gift from a childhood sweetheart, but he couldn't remember which one. 'I gazed at the words, conscience-stricken, "Forget-me-not". And I had forgotten.'

Forget-me-not (*Myosotis*)

Geranium *(Pelargonium)*

GERANIUM

Oak-leaf – True Friendship ❋ *Pencil-leaf - Ingenuity*
Wild – Steadfast Piety ❋ *Scarlet – Stupidity*

The geranium is a heart-warming plant, a spot of cheer on a kitchen windowsill; in its wild, true form, a gentle presence on a windswept hillside. When its flowers drop, the exposed fruit is revealed to be pointed in shape, like a crane's bill. The Greeks noticed this resemblance to the bird and called the flower *geranion*, from *geranos*, meaning 'crane'.

'True friendship' was the emblem assigned to the oak-leaf geranium, perhaps in reference to the strength and duration of the oak tree; the exquisite and skilful patterning of veins on the pencil-leaf flower brought the notion of ingenuity to mind; and the wild geranium, sometimes called herb Robert, a hardy little plant which often grows in the most difficult terrain, was also given a noble meaning; but the scarlet geranium was not so fortunate.

It acquired its emblem from a story of Madame de Staël, the eighteenth-century author and intellectual, and her encounter with a handsome Swiss army officer in full scarlet regimentals. After spending an hour with him, in which time he hardly said a word, she asked him questions he could not refuse to answer, and his replies were noticeably lacking in intelligence. Vexed at having wasted her time, she turned to the friend who had introduced the officer and said, 'Truly sir, you are like my gardener, who thought to do me a favour by bringing me this morning a pot of geraniums; but I tell you I sent the flowers away and told him never to bring them again. And why? Because the geranium is a flower well-clad in scarlet: so long as we look at it, it pleases the eye, but when we press it lightly it emits a disagreeable odour.'

Many Victorians, however, liked the scarlet geranium exactly because of its show of bright colour. Introduced from South Africa, along with numerous other varieties, it was grown everywhere, in fashionable parterres and homely window boxes – a cottage exotic. Miss Mary Mitford, the author of *Our Village*, a portrait of English rural life in the early nineteenth century, grew geraniums around a wire pyramid in a fine display. A tasteful dinner-party arrangement might include trailing geraniums and ferns cascading down from a bowl held aloft on a glass stem, or water-filled specimen glasses with sweet-scented geranium leaves floating on the top. The gift of an oak-leaf geranium would seal a friendship.

Oh! emblem of that steadfast mind,
Which, through the varying scenes of life,
By genuine piety refined,
Holds on its way 'midst noise and strife.

Though dark the impending tempest lour,
The path of duty it espies,
Calm 'midst the whirlwind and the shower,
Thankful when brighter hours arise.

Oh! could our darkened minds discern,
In thy sweet form this lesson plain,
Could we it practically learn,
Herb Robert would not bloom in vain.

ANON.

HAZEL

Reconciliation

Slender and resourceful, this ancient tree has served man since earliest times. It is fresh and green in the spring, its catkins a source of delight, then handsome in its autumn leaf, abundant with sweet hazelnuts.

The emblem of the hazel is 'reconciliation', a meaning that has its origins in the story of Apollo and Mercury, who first brought peace and harmony to the world. In ancient times, they observed the chaos in which man lived – without rules, religion or reason – and decided to descend to earth. Accompanied by his lyre, Apollo sang of love, and all who fought were reconciled. Mercury carried a hazel stick and touched each man with it, giving them the power of language and eloquence, the tools of diplomacy. In many depictions he is shown carrying his hazel staff, entwined with two serpents.

In *Little Hazel, the King's Messenger*, a book for children written by Matilda Horsburgh in 1876, the heroine of the story, Hazel Hope, does good deeds and wins people's hearts. The finest deed this 'little nut-brown maid' performs is to reconcile her great-uncle and his only son, who quarrelled many years ago about the son's selfish ways. Matilda Horsburgh was a popular author whose stories delivered a strong moral message. She wrote another book that drew upon the language of flowers, *Little Snowdrop and Her Golden Casket*.

In Celtic legend the hazel has magical properties and the hazelnut is an emblem for wisdom. An old story describes the Well of Wisdom surrounded by hazel trees: as the nuts fall into the water, a salmon begins to feed on them, and as a result acquires all the wisdom of the world.

from Domestic Peace

Why should such gloomy silence reign,
And why is all the house so drear,
When neither danger, sickness, pain,
Nor death, nor want have entered here?

We are as many as we were
That other night, when all were gay
And full of hope, and free from care;
Yet is there something gone away.

'Twas Peace that flowed from heart to heart,
With looks and smiles that spoke of heaven,
And gave us language to impart
The blissful thoughts itself had given.

Domestic peace! best joy of earth,
When shall we all thy value learn?
White angel, to our sorrowing hearth,
Return – oh, graciously return!

Anne Brontë

Hazel (*Corylus*)

Heliotrope *(Heliotropium)*

HELIOTROPE

Devoted Affection

The name of this delicious flower is derived from the Greek *helios*, 'the sun', and *tropos*, 'turning', reflecting the heliotrope's habit of turning towards the sun and following its course around the horizon. The plant is associated with the sorrowful story of the nymph Clytie, who fell in love with Apollo, the sun god. Apollo spurned her because he was in love with another, and Clytie fell into deep despair, spending every day prone upon the cold, bare earth, her pleading eyes riveted on Apollo in his sun chariot. Out of pity, the gods turned her into a heliotrope, and so for all eternity she follows Apollo's daily journey, her love unchanged.

George Frederic Watts captured Clytie's yearning in his 1868 sculpture of that name, which shows the nymph metamorphosing from a cluster of leaves, straining and twisting her neck to catch a glimpse of Apollo behind her. Watts believed that Clytie's devoted, searching gaze also represented man's quest for spiritual enlightenment.

The blossoms of the heliotrope form clusters of small, delicate flowers, white or lilac in colour, and its perfume is surprisingly intoxicating. The famous French botanist Antoine Laurent de Jussieu discovered the heliotrope in its native Peru, where, on finding himself suddenly overpowered by a delicious fragrance, he turned around expecting to find a gaudy flower but saw only the handsome heliotrope. He was so struck by the wonderful scent that he collected its seeds and sent them to the royal gardens in Paris, where it was first cultivated in the mid-eighteenth century.

The flower was a firm favourite in France, and it would be displayed in the most precious vase in the house, or planted en masse in ornamental troughs. Its warm, rich scent is like that of vanilla, and if the fresh flower was not available a lady could purchase perfumer Eugène Rimmel's expensive fragrance 'Héliotrope Blanc' instead. A husband who sends his wife a bouquet of heliotrope, perhaps the variety 'Beauty of the Boudoir', confirms his faithful and constant love.

When a widow entered the period of half-mourning, usually eighteen months after her husband's death, it was permissible to introduce a little colour into her costume; grey, white and lavender were the colours she was able to draw upon. The lilac or white heliotrope made a perfect corsage, its sentiment the perfect expression of a widow's sorrow.

TRUE LOVE

No, the heart that has truly loved never forgets,
But as truly loves on to the close!
As the sun flower turns on her god, when he sets,
The same look which she turn'd when he rose.

THOMAS MOORE

HOLLY

Foresight

The holly is the loveliest of evergreens: with its glossy leaves and scarlet berries, it has a festive spirit, and in the darkest days of winter it encourages us to be of good cheer, to celebrate the continuity of life and to welcome all that is to come. It was given the emblem of 'foresight' because nature protects it with prickly leaves until it has grown high above the reach of foraging cattle, after which the leaves, now out of danger, lose their sharpness.

Holly has always been used as a guard against misfortune. Pagan Romans would send sprigs to friends to wish them good health in the coming year; in later centuries holly branches were hung from the eaves to protect the house and its inhabitants. There was a strong tradition of using holly to predict the future, and anxious Victorians could indulge in this pursuit to allay their fears. Tiny pieces of candle would be placed on the leaves, which were floated in a saucer of water; the candles were then lit and the success or failure of one's affairs could be determined according to whether they floated or sank. Nervous young maidens, who wished to know who they were going to marry, made good use of the plant too. Nine leaves of smooth-leaved holly placed under the pillow and she would dream of her future husband; holly gathered into a three-cornered cloth and knotted nine times would produce the same effect.

Holly played an essential part in the Victorian Christmas, wound round gas lamps and picture frames, and bunches of the berries, the stem twined with ivy, made for a festive table decoration. Slender hoops bent into the form of a crown and covered with winter greenery would arch over the Christmas feast. It was essential that all greenery, especially the holly, should be taken down before Twelfth Night.

CEREMONY UPON CANDLEMAS EVE

Down with the holly, ivy all,
Wherewith ye dress'd the Christmas hall;
That the superstitious find
No one least branch left there behind;
For look, how many leaves there be
Neglected there, maids, trust to me,
So many goblins you shall see.

ROBERT HERRICK

Many young ladies' magazines included seasonal features on Christmas handicrafts, including how to make a motto out of holly leaves. Letters would be cut out of the leaves, sewn on to brown paper or card to spell out a seasonal greeting, then brushed over with liquid glue. Berries could be made by coating peas with red wax. No Christmas card was complete without the holly, often shown as a wreath crowning Father Christmas's head, or as a small bunch suspended over children's beds to keep them from harm. The exchanging of this lovely evergreen, albeit in pictorial form, provided everyone with a talisman to take into the future.

'I send the old, old greeting tendered year by year, for a Happy Christmas and a glad New Year.'

Holly (*Ilex*)

Hyacinth *(Hyacinthus orientalis)*

HYACINTH

Blue – Constancy ❋ *Purple – Please Forgive Me*
White – Beauty

With its soft perfume and delicately coloured blooms shaped like tiny bells, the hyacinth brings the promise of spring to a season of grey shadows and glowering skies. When there is so little scent and colour in the garden, its presence is precious and must be truly savoured.

> *Thy leaves are coming, snowy-blossomed thorn,*
> *Wake, buried lily! Spirit, quit thy tomb!*
> *And thou shade-loving hyacinth, be born!*
>
> EBENEZER ELLIOTT

Classical legend tells us that the hyacinth took its name from Hyacinthus, a beautiful youth with whom Apollo was besotted. But during a game of discus-throwing the god accidentally struck Hyacinthus on the forehead and he fell to the ground, fatally wounded. His drops of blood were turned into hyacinths, the drooping nature of their flowers echoing his bowed head as he stooped in agony. It is said that the hyacinths were purple, and so that colour's emblem echoes for ever Apollo's tragic mistake.

The hyacinth came to Europe in the treasure trove of bulbs given to Europeans by the Ottoman Turks. These early hyacinths looked very different from the popular varieties familiar to the Victorians: the arrangement of flowers was like that of a bluebell, tapering to form a pyramid shape. But eighteenth-century cultivation packed the hyacinth with double flowers, thus retaining its beauty and perfume for weeks on end. It became a highly desirable plant, its bulbs fetching high prices, especially in Holland where skilful Dutch nurserymen bred hundreds of new varieties.

By the nineteenth century the craze had died down, and hyacinths could be obtained at a trifling cost, affordable by both queen and cottager. At Christmas time they would be brought from the greenhouse to flower indoors on the mantelpiece amongst the holly boughs and ivy. A small but exquisite arrangement for the dinner table could be made by taking individual hyacinth flowers and mounting each 'pip' on wire around a hothouse camellia, set against a spray of dark green asparagus fern. A Christmas bouquet of white and blue hyacinths would be a wonderful gift for one's betrothed; perhaps the white 'Queen Victoria' and the dark blue 'Bouquet Constant'.

The January 1860 garden column of the popular fashion magazine the *New Monthly Belle Assembleé* recommended the Hyacinth Bottle and Flower Support as being ideal for growing these flowers indoors. The slender bottle with bulbous base was nothing new; hyacinths were often grown in water, not soil, in these small glass vases, which usually came in a variety of colours from cranberry red to cobalt blue, but the supporting wire was an innovation, designed to support the stem with its heavy bloom and keep it all neat and tidy. Edward Prentis's painting *Morning Devotions* is a charming tableau of a young family gathered together at the breakfast table, the father reading prayers out loud, the two maids listening primly in the corner. Proudly displayed on the mantelpiece are three hyacinths growing in their pale green glass vases, but without support.

IRIS

Message

The iris is the floral herald, the bearer of good tidings and warm wishes: 'My compliments. I have a message for you.'

In classical mythology, Iris was the goddess of the rainbow, the link between heaven and earth. She was also the messenger of the gods; clothed in colourful robes, she brought messages of hope to mortals on earth. Like the rainbow, the iris possesses a multitude of colours, every tone imaginable, all delicately painted in sky-washed hues, and so its emblem, 'messenger', is an inspired one.

This flower is also the fleur-de-lis of the arms of France. Clovis, the fifth-century King of the Franks, won a significant victory thanks to the flower. He found himself trapped between enemy soldiers and what seemed to be a deep river. But when he saw yellow irises growing in the water, he knew it would be safe to cross. The emblem was revived in the twelfth century by Louis VII of France, who adopted the purple iris as his symbol during the Crusades. The iris became known as the 'fleur de Louis', and eventually the 'fleur-de-lis', and was taken into the English arms when Edward III claimed the French throne in 1339.

It is one of the oldest of cultivated flowers, in Britain since the fifteenth century. New varieties arrived in the sixteenth century, and the Dutch East India Company brought many more into Europe from Japan a century later. By the nineteenth century, the Victorians had a wealth of different irises to choose from for their flower gardens; they also knew the wild irises, found in woodlands and watery places.

The Victorians loved the strong shape of the flower, and it appeared on numerous fireplace tiles and as a bold image on domestic stained glass. One wild variety, the stinking iris, was used in the winter decoration of churches for its brilliant orange seeds, which lie in rows like peas in a pod. An announcement of a birth, an invitation to a dance, a token for a lover or a simple message of introduction, all could be accompanied by an iris.

A pleasant message will you bring?
The most pleasant will be the wedding ring.

In medieval iconography, the iris was associated with the Annunciation, when the angel Gabriel announces to the Virgin that she is to bear a child. In Hans Memling's 1482 painting *The Annunciation*, the angel appears to Mary in her bedchamber. In this simple and ordinary domestic interior, a vase of flowers stands on the floor, filled with white lilies and a single blue iris.

Iris (*Iris*)

Ivy *(Hedera helix)*

IVY

Fidelity

The ivy that clings to the wall,
Symbols my heart's love for thee;
The ivy clings closely, so does my heart,
To the one adored by me.
ANON.

We love the ivy green for its lustrous foliage, which wraps itself softly around ancient trees and ruined buildings. Nothing can separate it from the tree it has once embraced. The faithful companion of its destiny, it falls when the tree is cut down; death itself does not relax its grasp, and it continues to adorn the dry trunk that once supported it. Its attachments end only with its life. Such steadfastness is a sign of true love and great friendship, and so the emblem of the ivy is 'fidelity'.

Fidelity was high on the list of Victorian virtues, and friendship brooches, one of the most popular gifts of the period, usually took the form of a small metal bar entwined with ivy, and the inscription NOTHING CAN DETACH ME FROM YOU. A tiara of gold ivy leaves expressed the same sentiment. When she was young, George Eliot gave flower names to her closest friends: her old schoolfriend Patty became Ivy; Maria, her teacher, she called Veronica ('fidelity in friendship'); and she called herself Clematis, for 'mental beauty'.

In two Victorian paintings, the ivy plays a highly symbolic role. In Arthur Hughes's *The Long Engagement*, a young couple meet underneath a tree. The ivy growing on its trunk indicates a lengthy betrothal, yet their vows to each other remain strong and true. But in Philip Calderon's *Broken Vows*, where an anguished woman is seen swooning against a garden wall, the ivy that clings to it adds great poignancy to the narrative. Through a crack in a fence, she can glimpse her lover flirting with another, dangling a rosebud for her to catch. What use is her faithful character now?

from THE IVY WIFE

I longed to love a full-boughed beech
And be as high as he:
I stretched an arm within his reach,
And signalled unity.
But with his drip he forced a breach,
And tried to poison me.

In new affection next I strove
To coll an ash I saw,
And he in trust received my love;
Till with my soft green claw
I cramped and bound him as I wove …
Such was my love: ha-ha!

By this I gained his strength and height
Without his rivalry.
But in my triumph I lost sight
Of afterhaps. Soon he,
Being bark-bound, flagged, snapped, fell outright,
And in his fall felled me!

THOMAS HARDY

LARKSPUR

Lightness

A glimpse of the larkspur cannot fail to lift the spirit: it has a delicate and playful appearance with its bright, summery flowers and carries an irresistible air of frivolity. Its name invokes one of the loveliest of songbirds, and again the heart is lifted in recollection of that bird's joyful and seemingly never-ending melody.

It owes its name to the shape of its seed pod, which has been likened to a lark's foot. It was once said to be beneficial for the eyes, and bathing them in the distilled water of the flowers was held to sharpen and strengthen the sight.

The larkspur is the quintessential cottage garden flower, and was regularly included in the flower garden paintings that became so popular in the last half of the nineteenth century. These soft and gentle images of cottage scenes and country lanes portrayed the rural floral idyll in soft focus. In Helen Allingham's *Girl Outside a Cottage*, a cluster of blue larkspur grows by the path. The painting shows a young girl just turning out of the cottage gate; roses encircle the door, ivy scrambles over the cottage walls. Country flowers and herbs were grown not only for picturesque and for medicinal purposes, but also to hide the shabbiness of the dwellings.

The French painter Henri Fantin-Latour also tried to capture the essential quality of the larkspur in his still-life *Larkspur and Roses*, painted in 1885. The light in this image is beautifully soft, and the larkspur seems vibrant and real. Fantin-Latour's style was very different from that of the cottage garden painters, but was equally popular, such was the Victorian passion for flowers.

He added just a touch of Impressionism to the floral still-life. His pictures sold so well in Britain, yet they remained virtually unknown in his native France.

For those who couldn't afford a fashionable flower painting, there were other ways of bringing this lovely flower into the home. A lady could try her hand at watercolour painting, or making artificial larkspur from coloured paper or cloth, a popular parlour pastime. Or perhaps, far less demanding, adding the petals of the dark blue variety to a bowl of potpourri. A glorious summer nosegay might include a generous spray of the flower, and what a compliment – it would signify great affection, and would wholeheartedly convey the message: what a joy and a pleasure it is to know you.

> *Who does not love a flower?*
> *Its hues are taken from the light*
> *Which summer's sun flings pure and bright,*
> *In scattered and prismatic hues,*
> *That shine and smile in dropping dews;*
> *Its fragrance from the sweetest air,*
> *Its form from all that's light and fair; –*
> *Who does not love a flower?*

ANON.

Larkspur (*Delphinium consolida*)

Lavender *(Lavandula)*

LAVENDER

Mistrust

In summer, lavender is utterly enchanting: a haze of purple shimmering in the heat, bees in a frenzy to partake of its sweet delights before the sun goes down; it is a glorious vision not to be missed. But centuries ago, when it grew only in hot climes, it was the belief in those countries that the asp made lavender its place of abode. For this reason the plant would be approached with great caution, and was therefore assigned the emblem 'mistrust'.

Since earliest times, lavender has been put to use as a disperser of sweet scent around the house. The Romans added it to their baths for its sharp, clean fragrance, and the plant's botanical name, *Lavandula*, is derived from the Latin *lavare*, meaning 'to wash'. The Victorians considered it an old-fashioned flower, but nevertheless a deserving favourite and quite indispensable. It could be purchased very easily, from lavender sellers or from the ordinary flower-girl, but was rarely bought as an addition to a bouquet or for display around the house, perhaps because its meaning is such a negative one. Instead, conscientious house-wives would place bundles of lavender in drawers or behind books; young girls would slip some amongst the folds of their bridal trousseau. The dried flowers, sewn into bags of pink or violet net and tied with a velvet ribbon, could be given to a niece or goddaughter, and ladies would tuck small sachets of it into their corsets as a deodorant. Yardley's or Perks's lavender water splashed on to a handkerchief soothed a fevered brow, and lavender burned in the sickroom removed stale air.

LAVENDER SONG

Won't you buy my sweet blooming lavender,
Sixteen branches one penny,
Ladies fair make no delay,
I have your lavender fresh today,
Buy it once you'll buy it twice,
It makes your clothes smell sweet and nice.
It will scent your pocket handkerchiefs,
Sixteen branches for one penny,
As I walk through London streets
I have your lavender nice and sweet,
Sixteen branches for a penny.

TRADITIONAL

Lilac

First Emotions of Love

Ah, let me weave a chaplet for your hair,
Of pale and rosy lilacs, lady fair.
Woe to the lover who would choose a rose
That in its heart a stinging bee may close.
Or yet a lily, or a spray of vine,
Or any bloom that wreathes a cup of wine.
The flower I gather, love, for your sweet sake
Breathes love that neither time nor ill can shake.

Persian love song

The lilac is a perfect union of perfume, grace and delicacy. From the first purplish bud to the full bloom, all is in happy harmony, and there is no greater delight than the return of its appearance in spring. The pale tints of the blossom and its short and transitory beauty seem to evoke youthful femininity, that first flush of loveliness as girlhood merges into womanhood. It marks the beginning of summer and of love.

Lilac has grown in Britain since the time of Henry VIII, when it made its way from the Middle East via Europe. The name comes, via French, Spanish and Arabic, from the Persian *lilak*, for 'blue' or 'bluish'. In spite of its connection with exotic countries, it is a plant very much at home in an English garden and was well loved in Victorian times, often evoked in the literature of the day. In *David Copperfield*, Charles Dickens places the lovely and naïve Dora under a lilac tree when Copperfield comes to call, bringing her a small posy of flowers from Covent Garden. When Jane Eyre is first to marry Rochester, he tries to dress her in silk, but she decides her lilac gingham dress is far more suited to her youth and loving feelings.

There is no better depiction of the meaning assigned to the lilac than John Everett Millais's 1859 painting *Spring*. A group of girls sit under apple trees in full bloom. They have come to pick the wild flowers in the orchard and have stopped to take a rest. One stands out from the others, as she is half standing, and it cannot escape anyone's notice that she has a spray of lilac tucked into her hair. Its presence indicates that they are all awaiting, perhaps have even experienced, their first emotions of love.

In 1880 the composer and conductor Frederic H. Cowen wrote a graceful and very popular pianoforte duet for the lilac in his series of short musical pieces called 'The Language of the Flowers'. Its short epigraph reads:

> *I dreamed that love*
> *should steal upon the heart like summer dawn*
> *on the awakening world, soft, gradual.*

Cowen was known for his light orchestral compositions and for his many songs, with their graceful melodies and lovely lyrics, often about flowers and poetic fairy legends. His 'Language of the Flowers' duets included daisy, fern, columbine, yellow jasmine and lily of the valley, represented in harmony on the first page in an exquisite colour drawing.

Lilac (*Syringa*)

Lily *(Lilium)*

Lily

Majesty

The lily is a flower of great beauty and of imperial stature; bending down from its tall and slender stem, it seems to demand and to obtain the homage of nature. An emblem of excellence, it is a glorious flower and without equal.

Of all the varieties, it is the white Madonna lily that is perhaps the most revered. One of the oldest lilies in cultivation, it is thought to have been dispersed throughout Europe by Roman soldiers, who carried it in their kitbags for its medicinal properties. But in the Middle Ages it took on a more illustrious role, through its association with the Virgin Mary, a link to the old story of the Apostles opening her tomb three days after her burial to find it empty save for roses and lilies. There is hardly an image of the Virgin to be found where the lily does not appear; it represents perfection and majesty of the very highest order.

To many Victorians the Madonna represented ideal womanhood, and to compare a woman to a lily, or to adorn her with lilies, was to pay the highest of compliments: like Mary, she is supreme amongst women.

> *The lily is the emblem rare*
> *Of many virtues good and rare.*
>
> FROM A NINETEENTH-CENTURY VALENTINE CARD

Lilies were worn in the hair and pinned to evening gowns, either at the waist or at the bosom. An inhalation of the white lily in a vapour bath was said to improve the complexion, and maids who used Sunlight soap were assured that clothes would come up spotless and 'lily white'. A lady might pose for an engagement photograph with a lily tucked into her dress, and young girls under a more modish influence could have themselves photographed in diaphanous white gowns, holding the flower. The *Ladies' Horticulture* magazine warned, however, against the dangers of keeping lilies indoors in closed rooms, its scent being very potent: 'it is sometimes sufficiently powerful to produce asphyxia. Here is another point of resemblance to the powerful of the earth, whose contact with the humble is so often fatal.'

When the actress Lillie Langtry was still relatively unknown, society portrait painter Frank Miles captured her lovely face in three different poses and in the background is a series of pencilled lilies. The presence of the flowers reinforced the message of her excellent beauty, and she became known as 'the Jersey Lily' (Jersey was her birthplace). Cecil Beaton photographed her in 1928, the year before she died, and there, for the very last time, she was posed with white lilies.

Highly coloured oriental lilies had been cultivated in Europe since the sixteenth century – the Martagon or Turk's cap lily was one of the earliest varieties – and, as trade and travel grew ever wider, more and more arrived from China and Japan. When the golden-rayed lily, its white flowers spotted with pink and barred with gold, went on show in London in 1862, it was proclaimed 'the grandest lily that has ever been seen'. The majesty of these lilies was in the splendour of their appearance and touch of the exotic. In the scene in *Through the Looking-Glass* where Alice is in the garden of talking flowers, Lewis Carroll gives the tiger lily an imperious character. This lily is rude to the daisy, larkspur and violet; only the rose is her equal.

Lily of the Valley

Return of Happiness

Where scatter'd wild the lily of the vale
Its balmy essence breathes.

JAMES THOMSON

The lily of the valley delights in cool, damp places and dappled woodland, where its bell flowers, like scented pearls, are modestly concealed amidst a cluster of bright green leaves. Shady spots can sometimes seem brightly illuminated by this sweet little plant. In the floral language it represents the 'return of happiness' because its flowers are at their peak in May, the month of merriment when spring turns to summer and happy, carefree days come back to us.

The lily of the valley grows wild in most European countries, but is more commonly found in the cooler north. In pagan times it was considered the special flower of Ostara, the Norse goddess of the dawn. Its botanical name, *Convallaria majalis*, derives from the Latin for 'valley' (reflecting its lowland habitat) and 'belonging to May'.

In Britain the flower is associated with Whitsunday, or Pentecost, the celebration of the return of the Holy Spirit to the Apostles. Its secular counterpart was the national holiday on Whit Monday, when many a Victorian would take off on a 'lily picnic' to gather the flowers in the local woods, followed by dancing and refreshments. Participants in the spring festival held each May in Helston, Cornwall, called the Furry (or Flora) Dance, wore the lily of the valley as a sprig on a gentleman's lapel or upside-down on a lady's dress.

from THE SHEPHERD'S CALENDAR

The stooping lilies of the valley,
That love with shades and dews to dally,
And bending droop on slender threads,
With broad hood-leaves above their heads,
Like white-robed maids, in summer hours,
Beneath umbrellas shunning showers.

JOHN CLARE

Accompanied by white lilies and white rosebuds, lily of the valley made a joyous summer bouquet. Or it could be cut and brought indoors from the garden for its beautiful fragrance, or to adorn the Lady chapel of a church. It was sometimes called Lady's tears, its drooping flowers representing the tears Mary shed at the cross. It was a common flower on greetings postcards; and playing-cards depicting wild flowers, very popular with flower-minded young ladies, invariably included the lily of the valley.

In France the lily of the valley is called *muguet*, and is the symbol of May Day, *la Fête de muguet*, when sweethearts would present each other with sprigs of the flower. The tradition is said to have originated with King Charles IX, who was once given a bunch of lily of the valley as a token of luck and prosperity for the coming year. He found it such a delightful idea that he gave this floral offering to the ladies of his court every year. The tradition still continues, and every May Day the French present each other with bunches and pots of lily of the valley.

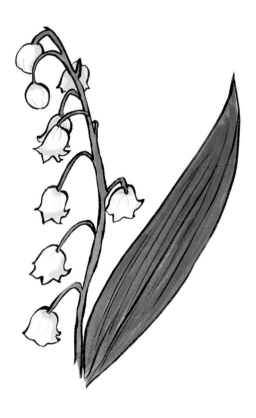

Lily of the Valley (*Convallaria majalis*)

Marigold *(Calendula)*

Marigold

Grief

The marigold is a bright and cheerful-looking flower, its colour a warm orange or golden yellow, its form open and honest, and yet its meaning is a sad one. But observe the marigold closely and the reason is clear. The flower remains open only as long as the sun is shining; cloudy skies and the day's end cause it to shut tight and its head to droop in downcast mood. Shakespeare in *The Winter's Tale* described it as 'the marigold that goes to bed with the sun,/ And with him rises weeping', such is the closing of the flower and its dew-drenched opening after the sun rises. Sadness and distress, the companions of grief, are signified by the marigold.

European gardeners have known this flower since the thirteenth century and the everyday variety, the pot marigold, was grown for its general healing properties, as a soother of many ills. Aztec marigolds from the Americas, sometimes called African or French marigolds, brought more choice to the Victorian garden, where the flower was admired for its hot colour and lengthy growing period.

In the language of flowers, the melancholy aspect of the marigold could be tempered with other blooms. Combined with roses, it could express the bitter sweets and pleasant pains of love; together with pansies it told the recipient, 'I am thinking of you in your time of distress'; with lily of the valley, 'You will be happy again, rest assured.'

A lovely image of the sad marigold appears in J. J. Grandville's 1847 *Les Fleurs Animées*, a book of playful pictorial fantasies based on the notion that the flowers have left the garden and adopted human form. The marigold has metamorphosed into a young woman, her dress a display of green leaves, her head wreathed in orange petals. She sits in drooping aspect under a weeping willow, feeling a little sorry for herself: 'All the flowers are happy while I am solitary, neglected and deserted without anyone to pity me.' Grandville, a caricaturist for French newspapers, was poking a little fun at those who took the language of flowers too seriously, but the fun was gentle and, besides, those who overindulged in the floral dictionary were the very people who bought his book and turned it into a bestseller.

MIGNONETTE

Your Qualities Surpass Your Charms

Tulips lack scent, roses have thorns,
On one my heart is set,
Come, blossom on my window sill,
Quiet, fragrant mignonette.

ANON.

To work in the garden on a summer morning amongst the hum of bees and the chatter of birds, and to catch on a warm breeze the perfume of the mignonette, is to know a moment of old paradise. Outwardly a shrubby plant of modest and unassuming proportions, it does not ravish the eye, but its sweet scent is magnificent and quite unforgettable, said to be stronger at the rising and setting of the sun. It is the virtues that lie within, not without, that are signified by this flower.

The mignonette is a native of the East, introduced into Europe in classical times, and was grown in the physic garden for use as a sedative: its botanical name, *Reseda*, suggests 'calming'. It had to wait until the nineteenth century before it was fully appreciated as a flower of distinction, and then its fame spread so quickly that no garden of taste was without its delicious scent. In France, where the plant was simply called *réséda*, the Empress Josephine had set the fashion by establishing it in her famous garden at Malmaison after Napoleon had mignonette seed sent back from Egypt, its natural home, when he was on campaign there. It first became popular amongst the French aristocracy, and then more widely cultivated at home and abroad; perfect for the balcony, where its breath of garden air would mask the smell of the dirty city streets.

By the end of the nineteenth century the mignonette was a great favourite of people from all walks of life; a garden-party delight as well as 'God's little comforter' in many a humble home. It could be grown under the window in a small garden or shown off to the limit in a Wedgwood mignonette planter. The cut flowers made fine evening posies and, slipped into a small vase, gave a delightful perfume for ladies' boudoirs or an invalid's room. Mignonette, heliotrope and white carnations made a perfect courtship bouquet: 'Your qualities surpass your charms, you are beautiful within as well as without. Sweet and lovely, I am devoted to you.'

from MIGNONETTE (LITTLE DARLING)
a ballad with words and music, 1895

Mignonette, little darling!
Ever dearest to my heart,
Like the flow'ret could I pluck thee,
Never from me shoulds't thou part:
While thy beauty kept its freshness
It would gladden e'er my eyes,
And when flow'ret like it faded
I would but the more thee prize.

Mignonette, little darling!
Heaven on thee blessings pour,
Mignonette, little darling!
I will love thee evermore.

SUCHET CHAMPION

Mignonette (*Reseda odorata*)

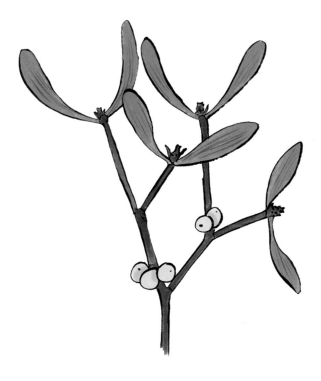

Mistletoe *(Viscum)*

MISTLETOE

I Surmount All Obstacles

On a winter's day, when the sun is low and the shadows long, the mistletoe is revealed in all its unearthly beauty, hoisted high in the leafless trees. It appears to have no roots, no means by which it can obtain nutrients and water, and yet remains fresh and green when everything around is lifeless. Surely it cannot live? And yet, against all the odds, the mistletoe flourishes.

The plant is associated with an ancient Scandinavian legend of the god Balder, who dreams that he is dying. His mother charms fire, disease, water and everything in nature she can think of, and makes them promise never to harm her son, but she overlooks the mistletoe because it seems too weak to do him any injury. But Balder's enemy, Loke, magics a mistletoe dart and slays him.

Ancient reverence for this mysterious plant bestowed on it magical powers, especially if it was found growing on an oak tree. The Druids worshipped it; it was believed to cure many ills; and because it appeared to grow spontaneously, women who wished to conceive would tuck a sprig into their waistband or pocket.

The Victorians adored the mistletoe, and like the holly it played a crucial role in their Christmas festivities. With other greenery, it hung in the hallway, around doors and picture frames; and on its own it would be hung up high for the favourite custom of kissing under the mistletoe. A huge bunch of it is suspended from the ceiling of Mr Wardle's house in the 'Phiz' illustration of his Christmas Eve party in *The Pickwick Papers*, and again in John Leech's illustration of Mr Fezziwig's ball in *A Christmas Carol*.

But every now and then a sense of the strangeness and mysterious power of the mistletoe would appear amongst the season's festivities. It was forbidden to include the plant in church decorations because of its old pagan associations, and this popular Christmas song, said to be based on fact, has more than a hint of the supernatural about it:

THE MISTLETOE BOUGH

The mistletoe hung in the castle hall;
The holly branch shone on the old oak wall.
The Baron's retainers were blithe and gay,
Keeping the Christmas holiday.

The Baron beheld with a father's pride
His beautiful child, Lord Lovell's bride.
While she, with her bright eyes, seemed to be
The star of that goodly company.
Oh, the mistletoe bough,
Oh, the mistletoe bough.

'I'm weary of dancing, now,' she cried;
'Here, tarry a moment, I'll hide, I'll hide,
And, Lovell, be sure you're the first to trace
The clue to my secret lurking place.'

Away she ran, and her friends began
Each tower to search and each nook to scan.
And young Lovell cried, 'Oh, where dost thou hide?
I'm alone without you, my own dear bride.'
Oh, the mistletoe bough,
Oh, the mistletoe bough.

They sought her that night, they sought her next day,
They sought her in vain when a week passed away.
In the highest, the lowest, the loneliest spot,
Young Lovell sought wildly, but found her not.

And years flew by, and their grief at last
Was told as a sorrowful tale long past;
And when Lovell appear'd the children cried,
'See the old man weeps for his fairy bride.'
Oh, the mistletoe bough,
Oh, the mistletoe bough.

At length an old chest that had long laid hid
Was found in the castle; they raised the lid.
And a skeleton form lay mouldering there
In the bridal wreath of that lady fair.

Oh, sad was her fate! – in sportive jest
She hid from her lord in the old oak chest,
It closed with a spring! and dreadful doom,
The bride lay clasp'd in a living tomb.
Oh, the mistletoe bough,
Oh, the mistletoe bough.

THOMAS HAYNES BAYLY

Moss *(Bryopsida)*

Moss

Maternal Love

A plant of immense variety, moss can be found in some of the most inhospitable spots, from barren ground to dank and dripping woodland. It takes possession of such places, covers them with its own substance and brings them alive. In winter, when all other greenery has deserted us, it remains to gladden our hearts and protect the roots of plants from chilling blasts. Birds value its softness as valuable lining for the nests they are preparing for their offspring, and in the summer, beneath overarching trees, it forms emerald carpets and softens the ground where we take our rest. Like a mother's love, it is a constant presence, it enfolds and protects and never deserts us.

> *Moss cannot boast of leaf or bloom,*
> *Moss sheds around no sweet perfume,*
> *Yet still we find her in the bowers*
> *In close companionship with flowers!*
> *In spring when Nature opens first*
> *Her store of buds so fondly nursed,*
> *Green moss on sunny bank she sets*
> *As cradles for young violets.*

ANON.

The Victorians gathered moss in great quantities for commercial and home use: flower-girls would line their baskets with it and wrapped it round the base of bouquets and buttonholes to retain moisture. A wicker basket lined with moss and filled with primroses would make a loving present from a mother to a child.

Moss often frequents tranquil spots and shady banks, and recreating these green and romantic places at home was a favourite pastime. Mosses and ferns would be grown in miniature indoor greenhouses known as Wardian cases, and dried and pressed for the herbarium. Keen collectors would take excursions on the railways to scour the countryside for rare and curious examples. For those who had to stay at home, a dip into George MacDonald's 1858 *Phantastes: A Faerie Romance for Men and Women* would conjure up the mystical and ancient places dripping with mosses and ferns that the Victorians found so appealing.

from MY MOTHER

Who fed me from her gentle breast,
And hushed me in her arms to rest,
And on my cheek sweet kisses prest?
      My Mother.

When pain and sickness made me cry,
Who gazed upon my heavy eye,
And wept, for fear that I should die?
      My Mother.

When thou art feeble, old, and grey,
My healthy arm shall be thy stay,
And I will soothe thy pains away,
      My Mother.

ANN TAYLOR

MYRTLE

Love

The myrtle is a beautifully fragrant shrub bearing delicate white flowers and lustrous evergreen foliage. Since ancient times it has symbolized the chief of passions, love, and according to classical tradition it has the ability to both inspire and retain that emotion. It was observed too that wherever it grows, it excludes all other plants, just as love, wherever it has established its domain, forsakes all others.

Roman myth frequently associates Venus with this flower, the myrtle bush having once offered her protection when she was bathing. In honour of Venus, goddess of love and marriage, Roman brides wore myrtle sprigs in their hair, and bridegrooms carried them in their hands. In Piero di Cosimo's *Venus, Mars and Cupid*, painted in 1490, Mars has laid aside his armour and succumbed to the pleasures of Venus's love. Behind his sleeping figure are myrtle bushes where cupids are playing with his discarded helmet and sword.

Myrtle has been cultivated in Britain at least since the seventeenth century, and was popular in Victorian times as both a garden and an indoor plant. Because it was a flower of love and marriage, it was frequently paired with orange blossom in the bridal bouquet. J. Perkins's 1877 *Floral Designs for the Table* recommended decorating the wedding breakfast table with chains of myrtle leaves studded with cyclamens. A young girl still waiting for her betrothal might send a lover a Valentine card of Cupid holding a sprig of the flower. In turn, a young man might gaze wistfully at Albert Moore's *Myrtle*, a painting of a young Roman maiden who looks him full in the eye, sensuous and inviting.

from The Passionate Shepherd to His Love

Come live with me and be my love,
And we will all the pleasures prove
That hills and valleys, dale and field,
And all the craggy mountains yield.

There will we sit upon the rocks,
And see the shepherds feed their flocks,
By shallow rivers to whose falls
Melodious birds sing madrigals.

There I will make thee beds of roses
And a thousand fragrant posies,
A cap of flowers, and a kirtle
Embroider'd all with leaves of myrtle;

A gown made of the finest wool
Which from our pretty lambs we pull;
Fair linèd slippers for the cold,
With buckles of the purest gold;

The shepherd swains shall dance and sing
For thy delight each May-morning:
If these delights thy mind may move,
Then live with me and be my love.

Christopher Marlowe

Myrtle (*Myrtus*)

Nasturtium *(Tropaeolum majus)*

Nasturtium

Impetuous Love

This is a flower that simply cannot wait. Once it has soaked up the heat of the sun and been watered by a little rain, it proceeds at a fast pace to cover the ground with its warm and colourful flowers and all-embracing foliage. It will grow anywhere and everywhere, and does not think for a moment about tomorrow, when the chills of autumn will nip at its tender flowers and all will be for nothing.

Originally a native of Peru, the fast-growing, hasty nasturtium made its first appearance in English gardens in the early sixteenth century. The flower has a sweet scent, like honey, and with carnations it made for a delicate but effective nosegay. Its hot, peppery leaves are reminiscent of watercress, and they would be added to other salad greens, sometimes with the flowers too.

Breeding and collecting introduced varieties with double flowers, and colours from scarlet red to pale lemon, but the familiar deep orange and yellow variety became the cottage favourite, and also a common ornament scrambling up trelliswork in small townhouse windows. In the 1860s the famous Coalbrookdale foundry in Shropshire began producing an immensely impressive and quite beautiful cast-iron garden seat they called 'Nasturtium'. The seat was made of wooden slats, and the back and sides were an elaborate scrollwork of nasturtium flowers and leaves.

O mistress mine, where are you roaming?
O! stay and hear; your true love's coming,
That can sing both high and low.
Trip no further, pretty sweeting;
Journeys end in lovers meeting,
Every wise man's son doth know.

What is love? 'tis not hereafter;
Present mirth hath present laughter;
What's to come is still unsure.
In delay there lies no plenty;
Then come kiss me, sweet and twenty;
Youth's a stuff will not endure.

'FESTE'S SONG' FROM *TWELFTH NIGHT*, ACT II, SCENE III

Orange Blossom

Your Purity Equals Your Loveliness

Bring flowers, fresh flowers for the bride to wear!
They were born to blush in her shining hair.
She is leaving the home of her childhood's mirth;
She hath bid farewell to her father's hearth;
Her place is now by another's side –
Bring flowers for the locks of the fair young bride!
ANON.

Of all the flowers – majestic, resplendent with colour or redolent of far-flung places – that could adorn a bride on her wedding day it is the sweet-scented, pretty orange blossom that is the favoured floral emblem. The spotless white of its blooms speaks directly of a woman's pure character; the uncomplicated loveliness of its form signifies hope for a happy future; and the fruit symbolizes the children that the union will bring.

The tradition has romantic origins, said to lie with Crusaders who, on having observed that Moorish brides wore orange-blossom garlands, adopted the practice when they returned to Europe from their campaigns. One Victorian horticulturalist declared he did not know why such a fuss was made of it, especially as the waxy petals gave the blossom a slightly artificial look, but he admitted that no bride would feel safely and truly married if she didn't wear it in some form on her wedding day.

From the modest Victorian marriage to the most wildly extravagant, orange blossom would usually be present: in bouquets and decoration, tucked into a straw wedding bonnet, and as 'The Orange Blossom Waltz'. A young man who declared he was 'going to gather orange blossoms' meant, of course, that he was intent on leaving his bachelorhood behind. It was often adopted as a pen name in the correspondence columns of magazines, and the advice to one reader who calls herself 'Orange Blossoms' in the *Girls' Own Paper* of March 1886 is quite firm: 'Your duty seems very obvious to us. Banish all thought of any ultimate engagement with the expectant widower, and at the same time certainly break off your own engagement. Would you perjure yourself before Almighty God? Tell him that you had made the painful discovery that you had been too hasty in accepting his proposal.'

Paintings and prints of wedding scenes were very popular in the Victorian period, such was the importance attached to matrimonial fulfilment. One of the loveliest depictions of the subject is Stanhope Forbes's 1889 *The Health of the Bride*. In this image, several generations of one family are seated around the wedding breakfast table, celebrating the marriage of a young sailor and his wife. The new bride, all eyes upon her, gazes down on her small posy of orange blossom, and a garland of it adorns her hair. Forbes sold the painting to Henry Tate, the sugar merchant and founder of the Tate Gallery, and with the profits he was able to indulge in a spot of matrimony himself, to fellow artist Elizabeth Armstrong.

When Queen Victoria married Albert in 1840, her wedding flowers were modest, consisting of a simple garland of orange blossom to fix her veil of Honiton lace. On their fifth anniversary Albert presented her with a tiara of orange blossom, the flowers made of porcelain, complete with porcelain stamens and leaves of frosted gold.

Orange Blossom (*Citrus sinensis*)

Orchid *(Orchis)*

ORCHID

Refined Beauty

Flowers of unparalleled elegance and grace, orchids are one of the world's great floral pleasures. Their delicate form and colour lend the plant a rarefied quality, but their impact is immense. Possessed of an almost hypnotic beauty, they draw in our gaze, which lingers but never tires, so exquisite is their presence.

Spotted orchid, lady's slipper, early purple and lady orchid (the latter named for the resemblance its petals bear to a crinoline gown) are some of the native orchids of woodland, marsh and meadow, and were well known and abundant in the Victorian era. But few of them excited the imagination as much as the tropical varieties that began to arrive in Europe from Central America, Africa, India and the Far East as empires grew and their floral wealth was plundered. By 1885, nearly two thousand species were in cultivation.

The Victorians were in thrall to the orchid: everyone wanted to possess a little of its elegant and exotic beauty. An orchid worn in the hair, an arrangement in a vase, an entire orchid house even – the flower never failed to impress, not least because it was so costly to buy. A favourite variety was *Dendrobium nobile* from the Far East: it was the easiest to grow and the most affordable, and its large pink and white flowers with velvety crimson splashes at the throat were said to have the scent of grass in the morning, honey at noon and primrose in the evening.

For those who found orchid-growing beyond their purse, a trip to Veitch's nursery in Chelsea, London, to walk amongst their vast collection would have to suffice. Veitch's was one of the largest growers in Britain, and one of the most influential, employing their own plant hunters to collect exclusively for them in the tropics and the Americas. A visit to their premises could be quite an experience: a uniformed doorman would greet visitors, and frock-coated and white-gloved assistants were on hand at all times.

As a gentleman's buttonhole flower, the orchid was perfect: it had the virtue of simplicity and its beauty ensured that the wearer stood out from the crowd. In Jacques-Emile Blanche's famous portrait of Marcel Proust, the young writer, pale and dandyish, sports a white orchid on his lapel. In *Swann's Way*, Proust uses the flower, the lovely purple-pink cattleya orchid in particular, to symbolize love-making.

from ORCHIDS

Exotic flowers! How great is my delight
To watch your petals curiously wrought,
To lie among your splendours day and night
Lost in a subtle dream of subtler thought.

THEODORE WRATISLAW

PANSY

Think of Me

Take all the sweetness of a gift unsought,
And for the pansies send me back a thought.
ANON.

The pansy is not a brash flower; it does not stand tall and proud, demanding attention. Instead, its gentle upturned face and petals the texture of the softest, richest velvet seem to ask only one thing: think of me, keep me in your thoughts. The French name for the flower, *pensée*, means 'thought' and reflects this flower's modest request.

In its wild form, the *Viola tricolor*, sometimes known as 'heartsease', is a small, scrambling plant of grassland and sandy soils, with three shades of colour on every heart-shaped flower, most commonly violet, yellow and blue. For centuries it remained unchanged in form, until in 1813 it caught the eye of Mr T. Thompson (his forename is unknown), gardener to a Buckinghamshire admiral. He crossed several wild varieties and developed the garden pansy with its much larger petals and a greater assortment of rich, blended colours. 'Fancy' pansies from Europe later added to the mix and the flower's popularity was sealed.

The pansy and the emblem assigned to it were of great appeal to the Victorians, who saw the flower as embodying the virtues of tender attachment, concern and compassion – the natural qualities of a woman's heart. A token for a friend would have pansies in it, as might a lover's gift, and delicate depictions of the flower adorned the front covers of photo albums. Mrs Warburton, a character in Louisa May Alcott's 1887 *A Garland for Girls*, explains why she is wearing a pansy brooch. It belonged to her elder sister, whose sweetheart gave it to her when they were about to be parted. 'This *pensée* is a happy, faithful thought of me. Wear it, dearest girl, and don't pine while we are separated.' Her sister is no longer alive, but the *pensée* continues to carry its loving message.

The pansy was also a popular motif in the Elizabethan era, known to be a favourite of the Queen herself. It appears on a pair of richly embroidered gloves from that time, alongside a weeping eye. The eye refers to the tears shed over lost or unrequited love, and the pansy signifies the hope that that love should not be forgotten.

from HEARTSEASE COUNTRY

Sister, the word of winds and seas
Endures not as the word of these
Your wayside flowers whose breath would say
How hearts that love may find heart's ease
At every turn on every way.

ALGERNON CHARLES SWINBURNE

Pansy (*Viola*)

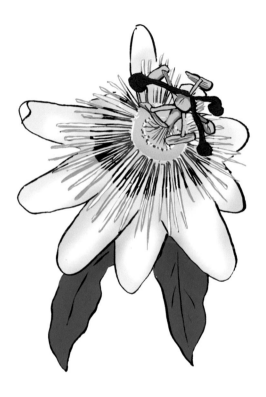

Passionflower *(Passiflora)*

PASSIONFLOWER

Faith

This lovely climbing plant entwines and embraces as it grows, offering sturdy support for its flowers and fruit. Its blooms can be found in a multitude of colours, more commonly a striking white streaked with purple. Their unusual beauty is fascinating enough, but more wonder is to come, for represented in the intricate structure of the flower are the mysteries of Christ's Passion. The central column is the cross itself, the five anthers the five wounds received, and the three stigmas signify the nails that secured him to the cross. The crown of thorns can be seen in the filaments that radiate from the base. It is said that nature itself is grieving at the crucifixion, and that the passionflower is the floral apostle.

This symbolism was first described by a seventeenth-century Italian monastic scholar. He had been given drawings and descriptions of the passionflower by Jesuit missionaries who had travelled with the conquistadors in South America, the plant's native land. For him the flower signified the triumph of Christianity, growing as it did in a non-Christian community: 'The flower is a miracle for all time.' And as European cultivation of the passionflower grew, so did its meaning as an emblem of religious faith.

The passion-flower, with symbol holy,
Twining its tendrils long and lowly.

Prayer and Easter cards were decorated with images of the flower, as were the bindings and title pages of prayer books and printed sermons. On Holy Cross Day, 14 September, the flower would be brought into the church in celebration, and draped around the font and holy statues.

Rebellious young ladies who refuse to go to church might learn from the lesson told in *The Passion Flower*, a novel of 1873. Young Myra Duval has inherited gypsy blood from her mother and a certain wilfulness from her father, which combine to make her a wayward character, resistant to religion. 'What can we know of God or heaven?' she declares. She follows her own passions and causes much grief to others, but finally finds happiness in the Christian faith and, to the relief of all, enters a nunnery.

A young nun contemplates a passionflower with some intensity in Charles Collins's *Convent Thoughts*. She is in the cloister garden and has been distracted from her reading of a missal by the natural beauty of the flowers around her. Perhaps she has had a moment of doubt, but nature, the design of God, has confirmed her commitment to her calling. 'I meditate on all Thy works; I muse on the works of Thy hands' was the quotation from the Psalms that Collins added to the painting's catalogue entry when it was exhibited at the Royal Academy in 1851.

PEPPERMINT

Warmth of Feeling

This little creeping plant is a lover of moisture and can be found in damp and shady places, woodland clearings and the banks of streams and ponds. It is named after the Greek nymph Menthe, who was loved by the god Hades and was turned into a mint plant by his jealous wife Persephone when she found them together. The peppermint leaf when applied to the tongue has a hot and aromatic taste, which perhaps accounts for the 'pepper' in 'peppermint', but is said also to reflect the warmth of love that Menthe felt for Hades.

The plant grows wild throughout Europe, and has been used since at least the seventeenth century for its strong scent and health-giving properties, especially its ability to calm the stomach. It was also said to stave off colds and influenza, and the menthol in its leaves could raise the body temperature and induce perspiration. Peppermint and other aromatic herbs bunched together would clear the head and sweeten the sickroom, but the oil that could be extracted from its leaves was its most valuable and useful property.

The Victorians knew peppermint in many guises, in confectionery such as mint humbugs, peppermint sticks and lozenges; as menthol cones burned to relieve cold symptoms; as a flavouring in snuff; as a tisane; and as a cordial, sometimes taken with gin to disguise the rough alcohol taste. Peppermint cordial, elderflower and hot water was a recommended cold remedy, while oil of peppermint was given to cure nausea.

If the small town of Mitcham in Surrey was the place you called home, then you knew peppermint very well indeed. It had been cultivated on a commercial scale here since the 1750s, and Mitcham became the centre of the British peppermint-growing and oil extraction industry. Mitcham mint was world-famous, renowned for its fine quality. Hundreds of local people were employed at harvest time and schools reported empty classrooms as the children went to work in the fields. (Prizes would be offered for regular attendance, but to very little avail.) Lavender was also grown in the area, acres of it, and the burning of the old lavender and the aroma of cut peppermint would hang over the town in a delicious miasma for days.

Peppermint (*Mentha*)

Periwinkle *(Vinca minor)*

PERIWINKLE

Tender Recollections

The periwinkle's emblem of 'tender recollections' has its origins in an episode in the life of the French philosopher Jean-Jacques Rousseau. When he was a young man, he lived for a time in rural and sensual bliss with an older woman. One day when they were out together, to her great delight, she spotted a periwinkle growing in a hedgerow. Rousseau thought little of the flower at the time, but thirty years later, long after their affair had ended, he came across a periwinkle again. All the tender emotions of that period of his life came rushing back, and the periwinkle was for ever associated with the happy days of his youth.

The periwinkle blooms in summer, long after the freshness of spring has gone, and its appearance seems heaven-sent. The simplicity and artlessness of its beautiful blue-violet flowers do seem to echo the clarity of our sweetest memories, so often those of our first affections.

The plant has grown in Britain since Roman times, and was once named the 'joy of the ground' for its trailing habit. It grows both in the wild and in the garden, where the Victorians would coax it to grow up and along a fence. As an emblem of recollection, it was planted near memorial urns and graves, and sometimes wound into the funeral wreath. Periwinkle was also recommended for the decoration of church windows at Easter, and along with yellow primroses could be studded into a cross made from moss and other greenery.

As the popularity of the language of flowers began to wane at the end of the nineteenth century, it fell to children's books to continue the floral education. In Eden Coybee's 1901 *A Flower Book*, an illustrated fairy story, the flowers are woken up in winter, just for one day, to pass on their emblems to the woodland sprites. Nellie Benson's illustration for periwinkle shows a sweet child dressed in a blue tabard, listening to the flower's message: 'I am early friendship,' says little Periwinkle, pensively. 'Even the very old on earth find comfort in me.'

AT NIGHT

Home, home from the horizon far and clear,
Hither the soft wings sweep;
Flocks of the memories of the day draw near
The dovecote doors of sleep.

Oh, which are they that come through sweetest light
Of all these homing birds?
Which with the straightest and the swiftest flight?
Your words to me, your words!

ALICE MEYNELL

Poppy

Fantastic Extravagance

'It is an intensely simple, intensely floral, flower. All silk and flame, a scarlet cup … like a burning coal fallen from Heaven's altars.'

FROM *PROSERPINA*, JOHN RUSKIN

When in bud, the poppy holds on tightly to its emerging flower; until suddenly, almost in the blink of an eye, the two imprisoning sepals are shaken to the ground and its floral glory is revealed. In a ravishing spread of colours, from blood red to deep yellow, crushed-silk petals shimmering in the sun, the poppy provides a show of extraordinary lavishness. Yet its flowers remain open for just a few days and then all is finished. So much for just a moment of splendour, but what luxury and infinite pleasure on the way!

The poppy's original home is the Mediterranean and the Middle East, but its cultivation in western and northern Europe is centuries old: the opium poppy was well known in the fifteenth century for its narcotic properties. Several varieties were grown in the Victorian garden, including strains of the wild field poppy and Iceland poppies from Siberia, but the extravagant and high-standing blooms of the opium and oriental varieties with their feathery and fringed petals were the most prized, especially because of their associations with the East, a land of colour, sensuality and visual spectacle.

This dream of the Orient was captured perfectly by John Frederick Lewis in his 1865 painting *In the Bey's Garden*. A young woman from the harem is gathering flowers; tall, rich red poppies are prominent, bathed in a clear, sharp light. Like the poppies, the woman is an ornament, an object for display, and the harem itself an enchanted pleasure-ground, a world far removed from the strict moralistic society of the Victorians. Lewis spent ten years in Egypt, far longer than any other Orientalist painter, and his greatest pleasure was to spend long periods camped in the desert hinterland under the starlit Egyptian nights.

Poppies

The poppies in the garden, they all wear frocks of silk,
Some are purple, some are pink, and others white as milk,
Light, light, for dancing in – for dancing when the breeze
Plays a little two-step for the blossoms and the bees:
Fine, fine for dancing – all frilly at the hem,
Oh! when I watch the poppies dance I long to dance like them.

The poppies in the garden have let their silk frocks fall
All about the border paths; but where are they at all?
Here a frill, there a flounce – a rag of silky red,
But not a poppy-girl is left; I think they've gone to bed;
Gone to bed and gone to sleep and weary they must be,
For each has left her box of dreams upon the stem for me.

Ffrida Wolfe

Poppy (*Papaver*)

Rose *(Rosa)*

ROSE

White – A Heart Unacquainted with Love
Pink – Grace ❀ *Pale Peach – Modesty*
Burgundy – Unconscious Beauty
Moss – Confession of Love ❀ *Red – Love*
Purple – Enchantment ❀ *Orange – Fascination*
Yellow – Infidelity

The rose is the fairest and sweetest of the flowers. Nature seems to have exhausted all her skill in the freshness, the fragrance, the delicate colour and the gracefulness that she has bestowed upon the rose. It embellishes the whole earth, is the interpreter of all our feelings and mingles with our joys and festivities. No wonder it is an emblem for love, the most important and universal of our passions.

For centuries, only a handful of varieties were cultivated – the *gallica*, the *alba*, the musk, damask and the moss or cabbage rose – in delicate pinks, whites and reds. But in the nineteenth century there was an explosion of newcomers, including yellow tea roses from China with their musky scent, and the prolific and highly fragrant Bourbon roses from France via Madagascar. As the century progressed, shades of orange, peach and scarlet were added to the spectrum.

The rose has been the emblem for love since the earliest times – the birth of Venus was accompanied by white roses; the medieval poem *The Romance of the Rose* guided the courtly lover to the garden of the rose, where he found paradise but the Victorians indulged in its symbolism and sentiment like no other, with a repertoire broad enough to express love in all its many guises.

The floral language of the rose needed to be carefully studied before any move could be made. The stronger the affection, the deeper the colour to match: a white rose for a young maiden (a pink flush at its heart is her girlish blush) through to crimson for a message of passionate love. Yellow was rarely considered a good colour in the language of flowers, and was used therefore to denote infidelity. In the rose's budding and blooming is a parallel with the transitory state of young womanhood and the ephemerality of love itself; so, the tender rosebud for a girl but the full-blown bloom for a woman whose beauty is at its zenith. The path of love from its first stirrings to its mature, sensual pleasures and the end of the affair – all permutations could be covered.

WOMEN AND ROSES

I dream of a red-rose tree.
And which of its roses three
Is the dearest rose to me?

Round and round, like a dance of snow
In a dazzling drift, as its guardians, go
Floating the women faded for ages,
Sculptured in stone, on the poet's pages.
Then follow women fresh and gay,
Living and loving and loved to-day.
Last, in the rear, flee the multitude of maidens,
Beauties yet unborn. And all, to one cadence,
They circle their rose in my rose tree.

ROBERT BROWNING

From the old moss rose to the newest and best, the rose was never out of place anywhere in Victorian society, whether in the shopkeeper's back parlour or the smartest country house. It featured in summer bouquets and lavish displays, ballroom posies and Valentine messages. Pale pink moss roses (with their abundance of petals, they were styled 'the ambassador of love' and declared one's passion) and a fringe of forget-me-nots could not fail to touch the heart. But if love needed a gentle nudge, then a stroll in a rose garden in June might inflame the passions. The advice of the July 1835 *Literary Treasury of Science and Art* was to wait until Midsummer's Eve and walk backwards into the rose garden and pick a rose; store it in a clean sheet of paper until Christmas Day, which would keep it as fresh as in June; then place it in the bosom; whoever removed it was certain to propose.

In Thomas Hardy's *Tess of the D'Urbervilles*, the maidenly Tess decorates herself with roses, unaware that she has caused a stir. 'She became aware of the spectacle she presented to their surprised vision: roses at her breast; roses in her hat; roses and strawberries in her basket to the brim.' She quietly removes them and, in doing so, a stray thorn pricks her chin, a classic ill omen.

The cowslip is a country wench,
The violet is a nun;
But I will woo the dainty rose,
The queen of every one.

THOMAS HOOD

Rosemary *(Rosmarinus officinalis)*

Rosemary

Remembrance

There's Rosemary, that's for remembrance;
Pray, love, remember.

FROM *HAMLET*, ACT IV, SCENE V

An aromatic plant of gentle appeal, rosemary is a shrub of dark green, needle-like leaves, silver-coloured underneath each leaf, which flowers in every shade from palest milky blue and mauve to deepest ultramarine. It is, however, a plant of some potency: when it grows thickly its scent is strong and casts itself far and wide, and when eaten it is said to have the power to strengthen the memory.

This association dates from ancient times, when it was recommended as a remedy against forgetfulness, and students in Ancient Greece were said to wear a garland of it to energize the mind. The plant's strong, sharp smell does stimulate the senses and clear the head, and perhaps this is what lies behind the belief that it could revitalize the memory.

A native of the Mediterranean region, rosemary has grown in Britain since Anglo-Saxon times. Over the centuries it was highly valued as a strewing herb and for its antiseptic properties, often included in a nosegay, and thought to be a remedy against the plague. The Victorians kept it in their kitchen gardens, often leaving it to grow rampant because of its tender associations. It was common practice at funerals for each mourner to carry a sprig, which would then be thrown into the grave. And there was another reason to carry rosemary: as an evergreen it symbolizes the immortality of the soul. In France it was customary to put a branch of it in the hands of the dead, and stories were told of when coffins were opened after several years and the rosemary had flourished so much that it covered the corpse.

The Rosemarie Branch

Grow for two ends; it matters not at all,
Be't for my bridall or my buriall.

Robert Herrick

Although the practice was on the wane, it was not unknown at some Victorian weddings for a bride to wear a sprig of rosemary to signify that she carried to her new home loving memories of the old. And sluggish minds might remember any number of important facts if the hair was washed with rosemary hair tonic, or with rosemary oil. General vitality could be restored with Hungary water, a famous preparation made with the plant, to be rubbed on the skin. This ancient concoction, said to have been made for the Queen of Hungary in the seventeenth century, was famous throughout Europe as a cure-all remedy, a tonic and a rejuvenator.

SNOWDROP

Consolation ❋ *Hope*

The snowdrop is one of the first flowers of the year, appearing in the depths of winter. 'I am come to calm your fears; to console you in the absence of bright days and to reassure you of their return.'

The flower originates from Turkey, Greece and the Caucasus and is thought to have been introduced to Britain early in the reign of Elizabeth I. The Victorians considered it unlucky to bring snowdrops into the house and so this was a flower that stayed in the garden. There developed a mania for the snowdrop, and many famous 'snowdrop walks' on country estates have their origins in the nineteenth century, when large numbers were planted to create impressive woodland garden displays, often to show off the rare varieties introduced by Victorian plant collectors. Some varieties were also brought back by soldiers returning from the Crimean War, such as the snowdrops on the Isle of Skye, said to have been first planted by Highland soldiers newly returned from the Crimea battlefields.

A brooch in the shape of a snowdrop might be given to a friend who has suffered a loss. A small vase of the blooms lifts the spirits, signifying that happier times will soon return. And a basket of snowdrops on a New Year's card sends hopeful thoughts: 'Every blessing attend thee through the coming year.'

In John Everett Millais's painting *Mariana*, based on the character from Shakespeare's *Measure for Measure*, a woman has stood up from her embroidery to ease her aching back. She leads a solitary life, waiting for her lover to return. '"My life is dreary

– He cometh not!" she said. "I am aweary, aweary – I would that I were dead!"' Her only hope and consolation is the small snowdrop depicted in the room's stained-glass window.

THE SNOWDROP

Many, many welcomes,
February fair-maid
Ever as of old time,
Solitary firstling,
Coming in the cold time,
Prophet of the gay time,
Prophet of the May time,
Prophet of the roses,
Many, many welcomes,
February fair-maid!

ALFRED LORD TENNYSON

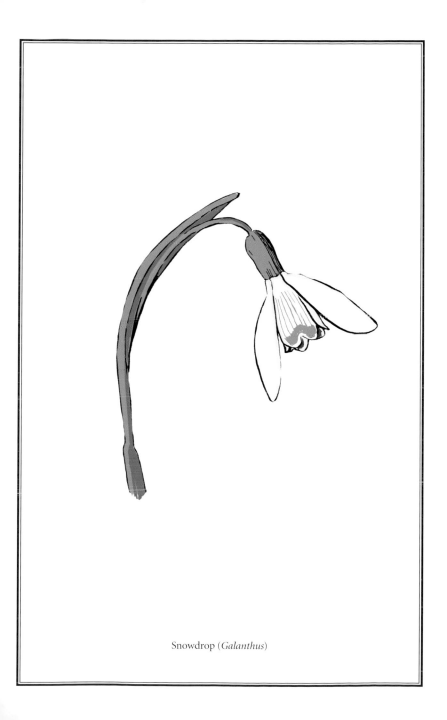

Snowdrop (*Galanthus*)

Sunflower *(Helianthus annuus)*

SUNFLOWER

False Riches

The radiant sunflower takes its name from the resemblance of its broad golden disc and surrounding petals to the sun. It was held in high esteem by Inca priests, and dazzling sunflower jewellery made from gold was worn by those who officiated at the Temple of the Sun. The first Spaniards who arrived in Peru in the sixteenth century were amazed at this profusion of gold, but they were still more astonished when they came across whole fields covered with these flowers, which they thought at first sight to be composed of the same precious metal. And so, for their bitter disappointment, the sunflower has been given the emblem of 'false riches'.

When the Spanish returned from South America they brought the sunflower with them, and this bright golden novelty spread throughout Europe. In North America it was much valued, especially for the oil that could be extracted from its seeds. It is said that when the Mormons left Missouri to look for land where they could live without religious persecution, the members of the first party scattered sunflower seeds as they went. When the women and children followed the next summer, sunflower trails marked their route.

And sunflowers planting for their gilded show,
That scale the windows' lattice ere they blow,
And, sweet to the habitants within the sheds,
Peep through the crystal panes their golden heads.

JOHN CLARE

Late in the nineteenth century the sunflower made an unexpected incursion into the world of advanced taste and fashion when it was adopted as an emblem for the Aesthetic Movement, a style of living based on the philosophy of 'art for art's sake' and championed by Oscar Wilde, Aubrey Beardsley and others. As a result, the sunflower crept into popular design everywhere, a bold and unsentimental motif, often appearing in terracotta on Arts and Crafts buildings, on wrought-iron garden railings, and on household items such as wallpaper, tiles and ceramics.

But many thought the sunflower too gaudy and vulgar for the garden and its floral meaning perhaps just a little distasteful, so it was eventually consigned to the cottage garden or an out-of-the-way corner. The Aesthetes, too, suffered a backlash from those who thought its followers false and superficial. George du Maurier, a *Punch* magazine cartoonist, pilloried them incessantly.

In one of his cartoons from 1880, he shows a family of Aesthetes, the Cimabue Browns, who are paid a visit by 'antiquated grandpapa (fresh from Ceylon)'. The room in which they sit contains all the familiar motifs of the Movement, including a Japanese screen and fan, and a tablecloth with an embroidered sunflower. Grandpapa wants to take the children to the zoo and the pantomime:

'Thanks awfully, Grandpapa. But we prefer the National Gallery to the Zoological Gardens.' *Other child joins in:* 'Yes, Grandpapa. And we would sooner hear Handel's *Judas Maccabaeus,* or Sebastian Bach's glorious "Passion Music" than any pantomime, thank you!'

THISTLE

Misanthropy

There is very little that is inviting about the thistle: its leaves are coarse and prickly, so to brush against it is to risk a sharp wound, and to tread on it is a painful experience indeed. The pretty purple flowerhead does have a sweet fragrance, much loved by butterflies and bees, but it is guarded by a cup of fierce spikes. There is no doubt as to the thistle's intention: stay away from me.

The reason for all this protection is clear: the plant wishes to discourage grazing animals from eating it. Allowed to grow freely, the thistle is hard to eradicate; if cut, it grows back stronger. When Adam and Eve were expelled from Eden, God said to Adam, 'Cursed is the ground for thy sake; in sorrow shalt thou eat of it all the days of thy life. Thorns also and thistles shall it bring forth to thee.' It was a popular belief therefore that the thistle was a cursed plant and a gift from the Devil. Little wonder that it was given the emblem 'misanthropy'.

from THE THISTLE'S GROWN ABOON THE ROSE

In Scotland grows a warlike flower,
Too rough to bloom in lady's bower;
His crest, when high the soldier bears,
And spurs his courser on the spears.
O there it blossoms – there it blows
The thistle's grown aboon the rose.

ALLAN CUNNINGHAM

Tough and durable, defiant against aggressors: the thistle embodied qualities that the Scots saw as their own, and the flower became their national emblem. There is a well-known legend of a Viking who stood on a thistle: his cry of pain alerted sleeping Scottish clansmen just in time to hold back the attack. The Order of the Thistle, a chivalric order founded by King James VII, has a famous motto: *Nemo me impune lacessit*, 'No one harms me without punishment', evoking the prickly aggressiveness of the plant.

In the January 1885 edition of *Ye Sunflower*, a Cambridge University student magazine written, it would appear, by undergraduate Aesthetes, this message appears in the agony column:

I knew you by the time, old chap, we parted,
And just this I'd say for those who have not that joy –
Their 'ignorance is bliss'.
I knew you better every day;
You're hardly worth a verse;
I knew you better, but must say
I also knew you worse.

SIGNED 'THISTLE'

Thistle (*Cirsium*)

Tulip *(Tulipa)*

TULIP

Declaration of Love

My heart is smit
With love so strong
I must declare,
But have no tongue.

Come to my aid,
Thou Tulip Red,
Go and declare
My love instead.

The tulip is so familiar and dear – our spring season would not be the same without it – that it is hard to believe its true origins lie in the hot and dusty lands of the Middle East. But in the sixteenth and seventeenth centuries, in the time of the Ottoman Empire, the tulip was as precious to the Turks as it is to us, and they had been cultivating and bringing it to a state of perfection for hundreds of years. It was a slim, pointed flower then, pinched at the waist, its image painted countless times on tiles and vases, usually in a beautiful deep orange-red colour.

Ambassadors of the Holy Roman Empire brought the tulip to Vienna in the sixteenth century, from where it spread to the rest of Europe. But it was the seventeenth-century traveller John Chardin who noticed the tulip's special role in the Eastern language of flowers, where it was employed as the emblem by which a lover makes his passion known to his mistress. The flower's strong, bright colour shows that the suitor is on fire with her beauty, and the black centre indicates that his heart is burned to coal, so fierce is the heat of his love. 'Beloved's Face', 'Slim One of the Rose Garden' and 'Those That Burn the Heart' were some of the varieties a lover could choose from.

The mania for tulips in Holland in the seventeenth century, when bulb prices reached extraordinary heights, made the European tulip a rich man's plaything, but by the nineteenth century it had become more affordable for ordinary gardeners. Tulip-growing was taken to great lengths in the Midlands and the north of England, where nearly every town had a tulip society and annual show. The growers were the artisans and workers of industrial Britain, who grew flowers on allotments and waste ground and in tiny back gardens. The Wakefield Tulip Society was made up primarily of shoemakers. Some famous Victorian varieties came from these growers, such as engine driver Tom Storer, who bred tulips on Derby's railway embankments, and Sam Barlow, manager of the bleachworks at nearby Castleton. Thanks to their efforts, love could now be declared with the white and purple 'Miss Fanny Kemble' and the salmon-pink 'Clara Butt'.

Tulip, or Two Lips, O which love I best?
The latter's much sweeter, it must be confest!
The tulip is grand and gay to the eye,
But Two Lips, when prest, will electrify!

A Victorian comic Valentine card is headed: 'Tulip – A Declaration', and beneath is an image of a tulip in a pot, its flower replaced by the head of a monocled and bewhiskered chump. 'All declare he's a perfect beauty,' reads the inscription beneath.

VERBENA

Pray for Me

In its wild form, the verbena is not conspicuously handsome, nor does it attract with a delicious fragrance, but it has a venerable ancestry and surprising associations with religion and magic. Known also as vervain, it was one of the sacred plants used by the Romans in their religious ceremonies; was said to have been used to staunch the wounds of the crucified Jesus; and was valued by the Druids in both magic and medicine, second only to the mistletoe. Many claimed also that it offered protection against witches and all manner of evil, and so the emblem 'pray for me' was awarded to this holy and honourable plant.

Verbenas for the garden first arrived in Europe in the early eighteenth century. These exotics from South America were tender little plants, but gardeners persevered with them for their vivid colours of scarlet and purple, providing a brilliant display of bedding in a fashionable parterre. Verbenas bloomed later than most European flowers, from August to September, so wealthy Victorians who went to London for the Season and returned to their country seats in August did not feel they had missed out on all the joys of their country gardens.

For those who wished to communicate the verbena's message, volunteering to work for a 'flower mission' would be one way of spreading the word. Nineteenth-century Christians believed that flowers spoke God's language, and the purpose of the missions was to distribute blooms to the poor and sick, the idea being that unfortunate people needed more than physical care, they needed inspiration as well. Flowers would be brought into town from suburban growers (the Great Eastern and Great Western railway companies carried boxes at half-price) for volunteers to distribute. The orphanage, the workhouse infirmary and the families of the deserving poor such as postmen and firemen, all would be eligible for the pot plants, cut flowers and nosegays. A Bible verse would be tucked into the nosegay, typically of sweet peas, pansies, carnations and verbenas. An 1879 *Illustrated London News* has a detailed depiction of a flower mission in action: a small image in the corner shows a forlorn-looking young woman carrying her flowers back home in an empty perambulator. The caption reads: 'A ray of consolation'.

Hail to thee, Holy Herb!
Growing on the ground
On the Mount of Olivet
First wert thou found.

Thou art good for many an ill,
And healest many a wound;
In the name of sweet Jesus,
I lift thee from the ground.

Verbena (*Verbena*)

Violet *(Viola odorata)*

VIOLET

Modest Worth

The Greek name for this pretty little flower is *ion*, and the word is said to have its origins in the Greek myth of Ia, daughter of Midas, who was being hotly pursued by Apollo, the handsome and athletic sun god. The goddess Diana, a protector of women, turned Ia into a violet to hide her from Apollo's lusty intent. In the wild, the violet does grow very low on the ground, its head downcast and concealing itself amidst foliage from the gaze of the sun. As a symbol for modesty and humility, it appealed to the Victorians' notion of the ideal woman.

THE LOST LOVE

She dwelt among the untrodden ways
Beside the springs of Dove:
A maid whom there were none to praise
And very few to love.

A violet by a mossy stone
Half-hidden from the eye! –
Fair as a star, when only one
Is shining in the sky.

She lived unknown, and few could know
When Lucy ceased to be;
But she is in her grave, and, oh,
The difference to me!

WILLIAM WORDSWORTH

This unassuming flower was extremely popular, the scented sweet violet and the Parma violet being the most sought after. It was so popular that it was grown commercially on a large scale, the famous Devon Violet nurseries supplying the London market. A woman might pin a posy to her dress to denote her modesty; or a Valentine postcard depicting the flower could be presented as a love token. The sweet violet is traditionally the real flower of Valentine's Day, not the rose. St Valentine was a Roman priest, executed for marrying Christians. In prison, he wrote a letter to his lover with ink made from the violets growing outside his cell.

The Impressionist painter Edouard Manet sent his sister-in-law, Berthe Morisot, a coded love message in the form of the painting *A Bouquet of Violets*. A posy sits alongside a red fan and a partially folded letter on which can just be glimpsed the words 'à Mlle Berthe' and Manet's signature.

Eliza Doolittle, the Cockney flower-girl in George Bernard Shaw's *Pygmalion*, is first glimpsed selling bunches of violets in Covent Garden; it was a staple of the flower-girl's basket, along with roses and carnations. The girls would buy their wares in the market early in the morning, spend an hour or so tying them into bunches and making buttonholes, and would then take off for their pitch, the entrances to hospitals and churches being some of the most popular places. In *London Flower Girls*, a painting by Bernard Evans Ward, the girls look healthy and cheerful, perhaps not typical of their kind, for flower-girls were desperately poor and prime targets for charitable causes. 'Flower-sellers breathe the sweet air of heaven, and handle nature's fairest products, but these girls pass their lives in sunless rooms, and seldom see a flower unless it blooms in some East End market,' was a comment made to the social reformer Henry Mayhew.

WALLFLOWER

Fidelity in Adversity

An emblem true thou art
Of love's enduring lustre, given
To cheer a lonely heart;
The emblem of a friend
Who in trouble will abide,
All needful help to lend.

ANON.

The wallflower blooms in late spring, and its warm, bright colours – orange, red and yellow, all intermingling – are an encouraging sign that the summer's heat is not too far away. In its wild state it is often solitary, and fastens itself firmly to walls or trees where it would appear that there is little nourishment to be had. It refuses, save when torn away by force, to quit its hold. When the first bloom is over, fresh blossoms are soon produced, as rich and fragrant as the first; it seems to know no exhaustion.

There is a famous old story about the wallflower; although the location varies from Scotland to France, this sad tale loses none of its romance. A minstrel and an earl's daughter fall in love and plan to elope. He sings beneath her window in the castle tower and suggests in his song a means of escape. The girl drops a sprig of wallflower plucked from a cranny in the wall to show that she has understood the message, but when the time comes, in her agitation she loses her footing and falls to her death. The distraught troubadour travels the land for the rest of his life, wearing a sprig of the flower in his cap. In memory of his continuing attachment to his lost love, the wallflower is the symbol for continuing faith in times of adversity, used by lovers and the religious-minded alike.

The homely wallflower grows all over Europe, wild and cultivated, and may have been brought over to Britain at the time of the Norman Conquest. It has always been loved for its sweet fragrance, warm and spicy like that of the carnation. It was used in nosegays in the sixteenth and seventeenth centuries, and again in the nineteenth in scented spring posies, in the May Day garland and as a delicious perfume. A few sprigs in an envelope sent to a lover would reassure, to a friend would convey continuing support. If a lady kept to her seat at the side of the room during a dance, whether from choice or lack of a partner, she would be called a wallflower, reflecting the plant's solitary habit.

Out of season, if there was a pressing need for wallflowers then Emma Peachey's indispensable *Royal Guide to Wax Flower Modelling* could solve the problem. With pre-prepared sheets of wax, metal pins and wires, sable brushes, colour paints and Mrs Peachey's detailed instructions, the wallflower could be recreated and enjoyed all year round, as could numerous other favourite Victorian flowers. This popular pastime needed to be approached with some caution, however: the paints contained lead and copper. Mrs Peachey recommended the materials she sold under her name and from her outlets, for example in the Soho Bazaar, which contained no poisons, and she assured her readers that they could indulge in the amusement in perfect safety.

Wallflower *(Cheiranthus)*

Water Lily (*Nymphaea*)

WATER LILY

Purity of Heart

*Fairest of Flora's lovely daughters
That bloom by stilly running waters.*

REV. FREDERICK WILLIAM FABER

The waters that run through our meadows or form quiet lakes of greenness host some of the loveliest flowers, the water lily perhaps the most beautiful of all. Its perfection is almost unreal, the white bloom especially, like a sculptured alabaster cup lying among glossy bright green leaves. The flower emerges sparkling and unblemished from out of the mud, pure and clean, ready to open in the warmth of the sun.

The Victorians thought it exquisitely beautiful and in the first decades of the nineteenth century, when intrepid botanists began to bring new water lilies back from India and South America, the fascination with them took a firm hold. This culminated in public showings all over Europe of spectacular South American lilies, including the Royal Water Lily at Chatsworth House in Derbyshire in 1849. Its leaves were so large that Joseph Paxton, gardener to the Duke of Devonshire, sat his eight-year-old daughter Annie on one of them.

Despite its fashionable status, the water lily as an emblem for purity and goodness was a theme returned to time and again. In Julia Goddard's 1884 *The Children and the Water-Lily,* a young girl spies a water lily, goes to pick it, fails and gets wet and muddy in the process. She is too ashamed to explain how she came to be in such a condition, and this sets off a chain of events that causes a great deal of trouble. Finally, all is resolved, and the water lily has taught her a lesson – that from the smallest actions great consequences can arise, and the truth should always be told. An artistic neighbour sends her a white china cup painted with water lilies and forget-me-nots: the reward for the pure in heart.

The water nymphs in John William Waterhouse's *Hylas and the Nymphs* certainly appear pure in heart – young, fresh-faced and surrounded by white water lilies – but appearances can be deceptive. Hylas, squire to Hercules, who has become separated from his Argonaut companions, comes across the nymphs in their lily pond, and they seduce him and lure him to his death. In this painting, Waterhouse subverts the flower's meaning, perhaps in order to shock. Just like the femme fatale, he is saying, the water lily may hide a dark secret: pure and harmless on the surface, but can anything rising from the murky depths really be so spotless?

from THE CHERWELL WATER-LILY

*To careless men thou seems't to roam
Abroad upon the river,
In all thy movements chained to home,
Fast-rooted there for ever;
Linked by a holy, hidden tie,
Too subtle for a mortal eye,
Nor riveted by mortal art,
Deep down within thy father's heart.
Emblem in truth thou art to me
Of all a woman ought to be!*

REV. FREDERICK WILLIAM FABER

WEEPING WILLOW

Melancholy

Slow wind sighed through the willow leaves,
The ripple made a moan,
The world drooped murmuring like a thing that grieves;
And then I felt alone.

CHRISTINA ROSSETTI

This is a tree with a mournful disposition: it chooses to live by water, a tranquil, slow-running river its favoured spot; its branches are pendulous and low; and when the wind catches its leaves it seems to be whispering sad and sorrowful things. The weeping willow's botanical name, *Salix babylonica*, is an allusion to the story in Psalms of the exiled Israelites, captive in Babylon, who sat by a river, hung their harps on a willow and observed that it appeared to weep as they did. To reinforce the tree's sad associations, it is also claimed that the scourges used to chastise Jesus were made from its branches, and that the tree has never been able to hold its head up since, drooping as a token of mourning and affliction.

The weeping willow's home is eastern Asia, and it was first brought to Britain in the eighteenth century. Thereafter it spread rapidly, planted in parklands and along the courses of rivers. The Victorians took to the melancholy sentiments surrounding it and absorbed it into their elaborate mourning practices. A classic mourning brooch would depict a despairing figure draped over a tomb, with an urn and a weeping willow providing the backdrop.

Perhaps an even more popular representation of the weeping willow was on 'willow pattern' china, at the time a stock design of almost every British pottery manufacturer. The origins of the Chinese tale on which the design is based are unclear, but its appeal lay in the fascination with all things oriental and anything to do with doomed lovers. Thomas Minton of the Minton pottery in Stoke-on-Trent designed and manufactured the pattern and made it popular. Other potteries copied the design and introduced slight variations, but the colours never changed – crisp white and cobalt blue – and the weeping willow, representing grief and sadness at the death of the lovers, remained the same, trembling in the wind, watching the tragedy unfold.

Two pigeons flying high
Chinese vessel sailing by
Weeping willow hanging o'er
Bridge with three men, if not four.
Chinese temples there they stand
Seem to take up all the land
Apple trees with apples on
A pretty fence to end my song.

ANON.

Weeping Willow *(Salix babylonica)*

THE EMOTIONAL DICTIONARY

~ A ~

abundance . . . . . grapevine (*Vitis vinifera*)

activity . . . . . thyme (*Thymus*)

advice . . . . . rhubarb (*Rheum*)

affectation . . . . . cockscomb (*Celosia*)

affection . . . . . pear (*Pyrus*); saxifrage (*Saxifraga*)

always cheerful . . . . . coreopsis (*Coreopsis*)

ambition . . . . . hollyhock (*Alcea*)

amiability . . . . . white jasmine (*Jasminum officinale*)

anger . . . . . peony (*Paeonia*)

anticipation . . . . . forsythia (*Forsythia*)

appreciation . . . . . lisianthus (*Eustoma*)

ardent love . . . . . cactus (*Opuntia*)

argument . . . . . fig (*Ficus carica*)

artifice . . . . . acanthus (*Acanthus*)

attachment..... Indian jasmine (*Jasminum multiflorum*)

audacity..... larch (*Larix decidua*)

~ B ~

beauty..... white hyacinth (*Hyacinthus orientalis*)

beloved daughter..... cinquefoil (*Potentilla*)

benevolence..... potato (*Solanum tuberosum*)

be of good cheer..... poinsettia (*Euphorbia pulcherrima*)

betrayal..... redbud (*Cercis*)

beware..... oleander (*Nerium oleander*); rhododendron (*Rhododendron*)

beware of excess..... saffron (*Crocus sativus*)

blushes..... marjoram (*Origanum*)

bury me amid nature's beauty..... persimmon (*Diospyros kaki*)

~ C ~

capricious beauty..... lady's slipper (*Cypripedium*)

careful encouragement..... goldenrod (*Solidago*)

caution..... begonia (*Begonia*)

change . . . . . scarlet pimpernel (*Anagallis arvensis*)

charity . . . . . turnip (*Brassica rapa*)

cheerfulness . . . . . gerber daisy (*Gerbera*)

childbirth . . . . . dittany (*Dictamnus albus*)

childhood . . . . . primrose (*Primula*)

chivalry . . . . . monkshood (*Aconitum*)

coldheartedness . . . . . lettuce (*Lactuca sativa*)

come down . . . . . Jacob's ladder (*Polemonium*)

comfort . . . . . pear blossom (*Pyrus*)

compassion . . . . . elder (*Sambucus*)

confession of love . . . . . moss rose (*Rosa*)

confidence . . . . . polyanthus (*Primula elatior*)

conjugal love . . . . . linden tree (*Tilia*)

consolation . . . . . snowdrop (*Galanthus*)

constancy . . . . . bluebell (*Hyacinthoides non-scripta*); Canterbury bells (*Campanula medium*); blue hyacinth (*Hyacinthus orientalis*)

coquetry . . . . . day lily (*Hemerocallis*); morning glory (*Ipomoea*)

counterfeit . . . . . mock orange (*Philadelphus*)

courage . . . . . black poplar (*Populus nigra*); protea (*Protea*) *cruelty* . . . . . nettle (*Urtica*)

cure for a broken heart . . . . . yarrow (*Achillea millefolium*)

cure for heartache . . . . . cranberry (*Vaccinium*)

~ D ~

dangerous pleasures . . . . . tuberose (*Polianthes tuberosa*)

deception . . . . . winter cherry (*Physalis alkekengi*)

declaration of love . . . . . tulip (*Tulipa*)

dejection . . . . . lichen (*Parmelia*)

delicate beauty . . . . . hibiscus (*Hibiscus*)

delicate pleasures . . . . . sweet pea (*Lathyrus odoratus*)

desertion . . . . . columbine (*Aquilegia*)

desire . . . . . jonquil (*Narcissus jonquilla*)

desire for riches . . . . . marsh marigold (*Caltha palustris*)

devoted affection . . . . . heliotrope (*Heliotropium*)

devotion . . . . . alstroemeria (*Alstroemeria*); honeysuckle (*Lonicera*)

dignity . . . . . dahlia (*Dahlia*), magnolia (*Magnolia*)

discretion . . . . . lemon blossom (*Citrus limon*)

disdain..... yellow carnation (*Dianthus caryophyllus*)

dispassion..... hydrangea (*Hydrangea*)

do me justice..... chestnut (*Castanea sativa*)

~ E ~

enchantment..... purple rose (*Rosa*)

energy in adversity..... chamomile (*Matricaria recutita*)

enthusiasm..... bouvardia (*Bouvardia*)

envy..... blackberry (*Rubus*)

everlasting love..... baby's breath (*Gypsophila paniculata*)

~ F ~

faith..... passionflower (*Passiflora*)

false riches..... sunflower (*Helianthus annuus*)

fame..... trumpet vine (*Campsis radicans*)

fantastic extravagance..... poppy (*Papaver*)

fantasy..... Queen Anne's lace (*Ammi majus*)

farewell . . . . . Michaelmas daisy (*Aster amellus*)

fascination . . . . . orange rose (*Rosa*)

festivity . . . . . parsley (*Petroselinum crispum*)

fidelity . . . . . ivy (*Hedera helix*); speedwell (*Veronica*)

fidelity in adversity . . . . . wallflower (*Cheiranthus*)

first emotions of love . . . . . lilac (*Syringa*)

foolishness . . . . . pomegranate (*Punica granatum*)

foresight . . . . . holly (*Ilex*)

forget me not . . . . . forget-me-not (*Myosotis*)

forsaken . . . . . anemone (*Anemone*)

fragile and ephemeral passion . . . . . azalea (*Rhododendron*)

frugality . . . . . chicory (*Cichorium intybus*)

~ G ~

gallantry . . . . . Sweet William (*Dianthus barbatus*)

generosity . . . . . orange (*Citrus sinensis*)

glory and success . . . . . laurel (*Laurus nobilis*)

good health and long life . . . . . sage (*Salvia officinalis*)

good luck . . . . . bells of Ireland (*Moluccella laevis*) grace . . . . . pink rose (*Rosa*)

gratitude . . . . . agrimony (*Agrimonia*);
bellflower (*Campanula*)

grief . . . . . aloe (*Aloe vera*); marigold
(*Calendula*)

~ H ~

happiness in marriage . . . . . stephanotis (*Stephanotis
floribunda*)

hate . . . . . basil (*Ocimum basilicum*)

heart unacquainted with love . . . . . white rose (*Rosa*)

hidden worth . . . . . coriander (*Coriandrum
sativum*)

honesty . . . . . honesty (*Lunaria annua*)

hope . . . . . hawthorn (*Crataegus
monogyna*); snowdrop
(*Galanthus*)

hopeless but not helpless . . . . . love-lies-bleeding
(*Amaranthus caudatus*)

humble love . . . . . fuchsia (*Fuchsia*)

humility . . . . . broom (*Cytisus*)

~ I ~

I am hurt . . . . . mustard (*Brassica*)

I am your captive . . . . . peach blossom (*Prunus persica*)

I cannot be with you . . . . . striped carnation (*Dianthus caryophyllus*)

I change but in death . . . . . bay leaf (*Laurus nobilis*)

I cling to thee . . . . . vetch (*Vicia*)

I declare war against you . . . . . tansy (*Tanacetum*)

I feel your kindness . . . . . flax (*Linum usitatissimum*)

I have loved you and you have not known it . . . . . clove (*Syzygium aromaticum*)

ill-tempered . . . . . crab-apple blossom (*Malus hupehensis/Malus sylvestris*)

imagination . . . . . lupin (*Lupinus*)

immortality . . . . . amaranth (*Amaranthus*)

I mourn your absence . . . . . zinnia (*Zinnia*)

impatience . . . . . impatiens (*Impatiens*)

impermanence . . . . cherry blossom (*Prunus cerasus/Prunus serrulata*)

impetuous love . . . . . nasturtium (*Tropaeolum majus*)

inconstancy . . . . . evening primrose (*Oenothera*)

indifference . . . . . candytuft (*Iberis*)

indiscretion . . . . . almond blossom (*Amygdalus communis*) infidelity..... yellow rose (*Rosa*)

ingenuity..... pencil-leaf geranium
(*Pelargonium*)

ingratitude..... buttercup (*Ranunculus acris*)

innocence..... daisy (*Bellis*)

insincerity..... foxglove (*Digitalis purpurea*)

inspiration..... angelica (*Angelica
pachycarpa*)

intrinsic worth..... gentian (*Gentiana*)

I surmount all obstacles..... mistletoe (*Viscum*)

I will never forget you..... pink carnation (*Dianthus
caryophyllus*)

I will try again..... liatris (*Liatris*)

I would not have you
otherwise..... daphne (*Daphne*)

I wound to heal..... eglantine (*Rosa rubiginosa*)

~ J ~

joy..... oregano (*Origanum vulgare*)

joy in love and life..... cosmos (*Cosmos bipinnatus*)

joys to come..... celandine (*Chelidonium
majus*)

justice..... black-eyed Susan
(*Rudbeckia*)

~ K ~

keep your promises . . . . . plum (*Prunus domestica*)

~ L ~

lasting friendship . . . . . freesia (*Freesia*)

lasting pleasure . . . . . everlasting pea (*Lathyrus latifolius*)

levity . . . . . delphinium (*Delphinium*)

lightness . . . . . larkspur (*Delphinium consolida*)

love . . . . . myrtle (*Myrtus*); red rose (*Rosa*)

love letter . . . . . agapanthus (*Agapanthus*)

love undiminished by adversity . . . . . dogwood (*Cornus*)

~ M ~

magnificence . . . . bird of paradise (*Strelitzia reginae*)

majesty . . . . . lily (*Lilium*)

make haste . . . . . dianthus (*Dianthus*)

malevolence . . . . . lobelia (*Lobelia*)

maternal love . . . . . moss (*Bryopsida*)

mature elegance. . . . . pomegranate blossom
(*Punica granatum*)

meditation. . . . . abutilon (*Abutilon*)

melancholy. . . . . weeping willow (*Salix babylonica*)

message. . . . . iris (*Iris*)

misanthropy. . . . . thistle (*Cirsium*)

mistrust. . . . . lavender (*Lavandula*)

modest beauty. . . . . trillium (*Trillium*)

modest worth. . . . . violet (*Viola*)

modesty. . . . . calla lily (*Zantedeschia aethiopica*); pale peach rose (*Rosa*)

mourning. . . . . cypress (*Cupressus*)

my best days are past. . . . . meadow saffron (*Colchicum autumnale*)

my destiny is in your hands. . . . . camellia (*Camellia*)

my heart breaks. . . . . red carnation (*Dianthus caryophyllus*)

~ N ~

neglected beauty. . . . . trachelium (*Trachelium*)

new beginnings. . . . . daffodil (*Narcissus*)

noble courage. . . . . edelweiss (*Leontopodium alpinum*

~ O ~

our souls are united . . . . . phlox (*Phlox*)

~ P ~

parental affection . . . . . sorrel (*Rumex acetosa*)

passion . . . . . bougainvillea (*Bougainvillea spectabilis*)

patience . . . . . aster (*Aster*)

peace . . . . . olive (*Olea europaea*)

pensive beauty . . . . . laburnum (*Laburnum anagyroides*)

pensiveness . . . . . cowslip (*Primula veris*)

perfection . . . . . strawberry (*Fragaria*)

perplexity . . . . . love-in-a-mist (*Nigella damascena*)

persistence . . . . . euphorbia (*Euphorbia*)

please forgive me . . . . . purple hyacinth (*Hyacinthus orientalis*)

poverty . . . . . clematis (*Clematis*)

pray for me . . . . . verbena (*Verbena*)

preference . . . . . apple blossom (*Malus domestica*)

presumption . . . . . snapdragon (*Antirrhinum majus*)

pretension..... willowherb (*Epilobium*)

pride..... amaryllis (*Hippeastrum*)

profit..... cabbage (*Brassica oleracea*)

prosperity..... allium (*Allium*); wheat
(*Triticum*)

protection..... eucalyptus (*Eucalyptus*);
heather (*Calluna vulgaris*)

pure love..... pink (*Dianthus*)

purity..... lotus (*Nelumbo nucifera*);
star of Bethlehem
(*Ornithogalum umbellatum*)

purity of heart..... water lily (*Nymphaea*)

~ R ~

reconciliation..... hazel (*Corylus*)

refined beauty..... orchid (*Orchis*)

refinement..... gardenia (*Gardenia*)

remembrance..... rosemary (*Rosmarinus
officinalis*)

remorse..... raspberry (*Rubus*)

return of happiness..... lily of the valley (*Convallaria
majalis*)

riches..... corn (*Zea mays*)

rigour..... lantana (*Lantana*)

rustic oracle   dandelion (*Taraxacum Officinale*)

~ S ~

secrecy . . . . . maidenhair fern (*Adiantum capillus-veneris*)

secret love . . . . . acacia (*Acacia*)

self-love . . . . . narcissus (*Narcissus*)

sensitivity . . . . . mimosa (*Mimosa*)

separation . . . . . Carolina jasmine (*Gelsemium sempervirens*)

sincerity . . . . . chervil (*Anthriscus*); fern (*Polypodiophyta*)

single blessedness . . . . . bachelor's button (*Centaurea cyanus*)

solitude . . . . . heath (*Erica*)

spell . . . . witch hazel (*Hamamelis*)

steadfast piety . . . . . wild geranium (*Geranium*)

strength . . . . . fennel (*Foeniculum vulgare*); ginger (*Zingiber officinale*)

strength and health . . . . . purple coneflower (*Echinacea purpurea*)

stupidity . . . . . scarlet geranium (*Pelargonium*)

submission . . . . . grass (*Poaceae*)

superstition . . . . . St John's wort (*Hypericum perforatum*)

susceptibility . . . . . waxflower (*Hoya*)

sweet and lovely . . . . . white carnation (*Dianthus caryophyllus*)

sympathy . . . . . thrift (*Armeria*)

~ T ~

take courage . . . . . mullein (*Verbascum*)

tears . . . . . helenium (*Helenium*)

temptation . . . . . apple (*Malus domestica*); quince (*Cydonia oblonga*)

tender recollections . . . . . periwinkle (*Vinca minor*)

think of me . . . . . white clover (*Trifolium*); pansy (*Viola*)

thy frown will kill me . . . . . currant (*Ribes*)

time . . . . . white poplar (*Populus alba*)

timid hope . . . . . cyclamen (*Cyclamen*)

tranquillity . . . . . stonecrop (*Sedum*)

true friendship . . . . . oak-leaf geranium (*Pelargonium*)

truth . . . . . chrysanthemum (*Chrysanthemum*)

~ U ~

unconscious beauty . . . . . burgundy rose (*Rosa*)

unfortunate love . . . . . scabious (*Scabiosa*)

uselessness . . . . . meadowsweet (*Filipendula ulmaria*)

~ V ~

victory . . . . . spiraea (*Spiraea*)

~ W ~

warmth . . . . . feverfew (*Tanacetum parthenium*)

warmth of feeling . . . . . peppermint (*Mentha*)

welcome . . . . . starwort (*Stellaria*); wisteria (*Wisteria*)

witching soul of music . . . . . oats (*Avena sativa*)

worth beyond beauty . . . . . alyssum (*Lobularia maritima*)

~ Y ~

you are delicious . . . . . potato vine (*Solanum jasminoides*)

you are my life . . . . . lungwort (*Pulmonaria*)

you are near a snare..... dragon plant (*Dracaena*)

you are perfect..... pineapple (*Ananas comosus*)

you are radiant with charms..... ranunculus (*Ranunculus asiaticus*)

you pierce my heart..... gladiolus (*Gladiolus*)

your charms are unequalled..... peach (*Prunus persica*)

your looks freeze me..... ice plant (*Carpobrotus chilensis*)

your presence soothes me..... petunia (*Petunia*)

your purity equals your loveliness..... orange blossom (*Citrus sinensis*)

your qualities surpass your charms..... mignonette (*Reseda odorata*)

you will always be beautiful to me..... stock (*Malcolmia maritima*)

youthful gladness..... crocus (*Crocus*)

~ Z ~

zest..... lemon (*Citrus limon*)

Flowers for
Specific Occasions

Since time immemorial, we have given bouquets as gifts and
to express our feelings. We have also used the simplicity and
the natural grace of flowers to lend beauty and meaning to the
important events in our lives. We know that there is something
very special about flowers and that they have an ability to convey
certain feelings so much better than words; that roses signify
love, for example, that a bunch of daffodils somehow promises
better times ahead, and that to receive flowers in sympathy
both comforts and expresses sadness at the same time. Clearly
we do subscribe to a floral language of sorts, but compared to
the vocabulary the Victorians had at their disposal, it is a very
generalized and limited one. They would be aghast if only red
roses were sent on Valentine's Day, and quite horrified at the
modern belief that the showier and more expensive the flower,
the stronger the feeling conveyed. The classic Victorian Valentine
bouquet was sweet and simple: moss roses (more likely to be pink
or white, not red), forget-me-nots, violets and pinks. The message
was reinforced by the addition of a sprig of fern (*sincerity*).
The bouquet spoke of love, but also paid a compliment to the
recipient's character. On the surface it was a modest-looking
posy, but one that contained within it a wealth of meanings.

Using a wider and more varied language of flowers will require putting aside a few received opinions as to what constitutes an effective bouquet or display (size really doesn't matter, for instance). It will also mean calling more upon garden and wild flowers, herbs and tree blossom where the oldest, sweetest and most interesting meanings reside, but the result will convey so much more than the average florist's arrangement, and the recipient is assured of something heartfelt and considered, and nothing short of truly original.

There are no set rules stipulating which flowers must go together, and some of the meanings are open to interpretation; therefore no combination of flowers can be truly wrong. What follow are some suggestions to help the novice interpreter.

Courtship

The First Bouquet
a bunch of tulips (*declaration of love*)
moss roses (*confession of love*) and iris (*message*)
pansy (*think of me*) and cyclamen (*timid hope*)

The First Romance
lilac (*first emotions of love*), white rose (*a heart unacquainted
    with love*) and sweet peas (*delicate pleasures*)
white carnation (*sweet and lovely*), larkspur (*lightness*) and pale
    peach rose (*modesty*)

A Gentle Bouquet
pinks (*pure love*), gentian (*intrinsic worth*) and daphne (*I would
    not have you otherwise*)

violet (*modest worth*), pink rose (*grace*) and forget-me-not
(*forget me not*)
gardenia (*refinement*), burgundy rose (*unconscious beauty*) and
fern (*sincerity*)

A Passionate Bouquet
Use rich colours with bold shapes. The darker the colour, the
stronger the passion.
a mixture of coloured roses: orange (*fascination*), red (*love*),
purple (*enchantment*)
bird of paradise (*magnificence*), bougainvillea (*passion*) and lilies
(*majesty*)
jonquil (*desire*), tuberose (*dangerous pleasures*) and nasturtium
(*impetuous love*)

Rebuffs and Responses
goldenrod (*careful encouragement*), marjoram (*blushes*) and
aster (*patience*)
hydrangea (*dispassion*) and candytuft (*indifference*)
yellow carnation (*disdain*), rhododendron (*beware*) and
snapdragon (*presumption*)

For an Absent Lover
alstroemeria (*devotion*), dogwood (*love undiminished by
adversity*) and Carolina jasmine (*separation*)
pansy (*think of me*), wallflower (*fidelity in adversity*) and bluebell
(*constancy*)
zinnia (*I mourn your absence*), aster (*patience*), ivy (*fidelity*) and
Indian jasmine (*attachment*)

To End the Affair

a bunch of anemones (*forsaken*)

azalea (*fragile and ephemeral passion*) and cherry blossom
(*impermanence*)

striped carnation (*I cannot be with you*) and basil (*hate*)

columbine (*desertion*) and Michaelmas daisy (*farewell*)

Weddings

A Posy for a Young Bride

pinks (*pure love*), rosemary (*remembrance*) and stephanotis
(*happiness in marriage*)

lily of the valley (*return of happiness*), myrtle (*love*) and orange
blossom (*your purity equals your loveliness*)

pale peach rose (*modesty*), pink rose (*grace*), calla lily (*modesty*)
and stock (*you will always be beautiful to me*)

white hyacinth (*beauty*), blue hyacinth (*constancy*) and crocus
(*youthful gladness*)

A Posy for an Older Bride

gardenia (*refinement*) and lily (*majesty*)

myrtle (*love*), orchid (*refined beauty*) and stephanotis (*happiness
in marriage*)

red rose in full bloom (*love*), ranunculus (*you are radiant with
charms*) and lily of the valley (*return of happiness*)

A Country Flowers Posy

celandine (*joys to come*), crocus (*youthful gladness*) and daffodils
(*new beginnings*)

corn (*riches*) and everlasting pea (*lasting pleasure*)

honesty (*honesty*), pansy (*think of me*) and speedwell (*fidelity*)

DECORATING THE CHURCH OR REGISTER OFFICE

Twining plants with tendrils signify devotion and attachment.

wisteria (*welcome*), grapevine (*abundance*), honeysuckle
(*devotion*), Indian jasmine (*attachment*) and ivy (*fidelity*)

Tree blossom for windows and tables; include hazel to ensure
harmony in the marriage.

linden (*conjugal love*), hazel (*reconciliation*) and plum blossom
(*keep your promises*)

DECORATING THE WEDDING BREAKFAST TABLE

baby's breath (*everlasting love*), cosmos (*joy in love and life*) and
myrtle (*love*)

phlox (*our souls are united*) and parsley (*festivity*)

gerber daisy (*cheerfulness*) and fern (*sincerity*)

strawberries (*perfection*)

Births and Christenings

FLOWERS FOR A NEW MOTHER

dittany (*childbirth*), primrose (*childhood*) and celandine (*joys to
come*)

daffodils (*new beginnings*), baby's breath (*everlasting love*) and
fennel (*strength*)

FLOWERS FOR THE CHRISTENING

starwort (*welcome*), cinquefoil (*beloved daughter*), daisy
(*innocence*), eucalyptus (*protection*)

phlox (*our souls are united*), moss (*maternal love*), heather
   (*protection*) and sorrel (*parental affection*)

Illness

Small bunches of scented and flowering herbs for when the person
is still unwell; larger and brighter flowers when on the mend.
chamomile (*energy in adversity*), sage (*good health and long life*),
   heather (*protection*) and thrift (*sympathy*)
elder (*compassion*), fennel (*strength*), feverfew (*warmth*) and
   mullein (*take courage*)
snowdrop (*consolation and hope*)
purple coneflower (*strength and health*) and heather (*protection*)
coreopsis (*always cheerful*), peppermint (*warmth of feeling*) and
   hawthorn (*hope*)

Friendship

A NEW JOB
bells of Ireland (*good luck*) and allium (*prosperity*)
corn (*riches*), daffodils (*new beginnings*) and polyanthus
   (*confidence*)
hollyhock (*ambition*) and laurel (*glory and success*)
Michaelmas daisy (*farewell*)

AN APOLOGY
fig (*argument*), purple hyacinth (*please forgive me*) and hazel
   (*reconciliation*)

helenium (*tears*), olive (*peace*) and broom (*humility*)

TO SAY THANK YOU

agrimony (*gratitude*), feverfew (*warmth*) and flax (*I feel your kindness*)

freesia (*lasting friendship*) and oak-leaf geranium (*true friendship*)

lisianthus (*appreciation*), peppermint (*warmth of feeling*) and saxifrage (*affection*)

Funerals

FOR A WREATH

cypress (*mourning*), weeping willow (*melancholy*), periwinkle (*tender recollections*) and rosemary (*remembrance*)

The evergreens also symbolize immortality.

FUNERAL FLOWERS

marigold (*grief*), heliotrope (*devoted affection*) and aloe (*grief*)

forget-me-not (*forget me not*), helenium (*tears*) and marigold (*grief*)

Carolina jasmine (*separation*) and ivy (*attachment*)

FOR A CHILD

daisy (*innocence*), moss (*maternal love*) and primrose (*childhood*)

'A flower is not a flower alone;
a thousand thoughts invest it'

MANDY KIRKBY is an editor and flower enthusiast who lives in Cambridge, England.

VANESSA DIFFENBAUGH is a writer, whose debut novel *The Language of Flowers* has been published in over thirty countries. She lives in Cambridge, Massachusetts.